ELLA BAKER

*A Leader
Behind
the Scenes*

The History of the Civil Rights Movement

ELLA BAKER

A Leader Behind the Scenes

by **Shyrlee Dallard**

With an Introduction by
ANDREW YOUNG

Silver Burdett Press

To Jeanette

Series Consultant: Aldon Morris

Cover and Text Design: Design Five, New York
Maps: General Cartography, Inc.
Series Editorial Supervisor: Richard G. Gallin
Series Supervision of Art and Design: Leslie Bauman
Series Editing: Agincourt Press
Concept Editor: Della Rowland

Consultants: Debra M. Hall, Design Editor, American Library Association, Chicago, Illinois; Fath Ruffins, Historian, National Museum of American History, Smithsonian Institution, Washington, D.C.

Library of Congress Cataloging-in-Publication Data

Dallard, Shyrlee.
   Ella Baker: a leader behind the scenes / by Shyrlee Dallard; with an introduction by Andrew Young.
      p.   cm. —(The History of the civil rights movement)
   Includes bibliographical references and index.
   Summary: Examines the life of the civil rights worker who organized for freedom and was a key figure in the formation of the Student Nonviolent Coordinating Committee, the Southern Christian Leadership Conference, and other civil rights organizations.
      1. Baker, Ella, 1903-1986—Juvenile literature. 2. Afro-Americans—Biography—Juvenile literature. 3. Civil rights workers—United States—Biography—Juvenile literature. 4. Civil rights movements—United States—History—20th century—Juvenile literature. 5. Afro-Americans—Civil rights—Juvenile literature. [1. Baker, Ella, 1903-1986. 2. Civil rights workers. 3. Afro-Americans—Biography.] I. Title. II. Series.
E185.97.B214D35   1990
323'.092—dc20
[B]   90-31932
[92]   CIP
                                                                                              AC

ISBN 0-382-09931-1 (lib bdg.)
      0-382-24066-9 (pbk.)

CONTENTS

INTRODUCTION
By Andrew Young

Some thirty years ago, a peaceful revolution took place in the United States, as African Americans sought equal rights. That revolution, which occurred between 1954 and 1968, is called the civil rights movement. Actually, African Americans have been struggling for their civil rights for as long as they have been in this country. Before the Civil War, brave abolitionists were calling out for an end to the injustice and cruelty of slavery. Even after the Civil War freed slaves, African Americans were still forced to fight other forms of racism and discrimination—segregation and prejudice. This movement still continues today as people of color battle racial hatred and economic exploitation all over the world.

The books in this series tell the stories of the lives of Ella Baker, Stokely Carmichael, Fannie Lou Hamer, Jesse Jackson, Malcolm X, Thurgood Marshall, Rosa Parks, A. Philip Randolph, and Martin Luther King, Jr.—just a few of the thousands of brave people who worked in the civil rights movement. Learning about these heroes is an important lesson in American history. They risked their homes and their jobs—and some gave their lives—to secure rights and freedoms that we now enjoy and often take for granted.

Most of us know the name of Dr. Martin Luther King, Jr., the nonviolent leader of the movement. But others who were just as important may not be as familiar. Rosa Parks insisted on her right to a seat on a public bus. Her action started a bus boycott that changed a segregation law and sparked a movement.

Ella Baker was instrumental in founding two major civil rights organizations, the Southern Christian Leadership Conference (SCLC) and the Student Nonviolent Coordinating Committee (SNCC). One of the chairpersons of SNCC, Stokely Carmichael, is perhaps best known for making the slogan "Black Power" famous. Malcolm X, the strong voice from the urban north, rose from a prison inmate to a powerful black Muslim leader.

Not many people know that the main organizer of the 1963 March on Washington was A. Philip Randolph. Younger leaders called Randolph the "father of the movement." Fannie Lou Hamer, a poor sharecropper from Mississippi, was such a powerful speaker for voters rights that President Lyndon Johnson blocked out television coverage of the 1964 Democratic National Convention to keep her off the air. Thurgood Marshall was the first African American to be made a Supreme Court justice.

Many who demanded equality paid for their actions. They were fired from their jobs, thrown out of their homes, beaten, and even killed. But they marched, went to jail, and put their lives on the line over and over again for the right to equal justice. These rights include something as simple as being able to sit and eat at a lunch counter. They include political rights such as the right to vote. They also include the equal rights to education and job opportunities that lead to economic betterment.

We are now approaching a level of democracy that allows all citizens of the United States to participate in the American dream. Jesse Jackson, for example, has pursued the dream of the highest office in this land, the president of the United States. Jackson's running for president was made possible by those who went before him. They are the people whose stories are included in this biography and history series, as well as thousands of others who remain nameless. They are people who depend upon you to carry on the dream of liberty and justice for all people of the world.

Civil Rights Movement Time Line

—1954———1955———1956———1957—

May 17—
Brown v. *Board of Education of Topeka I:* Supreme Court rules racial segregation in public is unconstitutional.

May 31—
Brown v. *Board of Education of Topeka II:* Supreme Court says desegregation of public schools must proceed "with all deliberate speed."

August 28—
14-year-old Emmett Till is killed in Money, Mississippi.

December 5, 1955–December 20, 1956—
Montgomery, Alabama bus boycott.

November 13—
Supreme Court outlaws racial segregation on Alabama's city buses.

January 10, 11—
Southern Christian Leadership Conference (SCLC) is founded.

August 29—
Civil Rights Act is passed. Among other things, it creates Civil Rights Commission to advise the president and gives government power to uphold voting rights.

September 1957–
Little Rock Central High School is desegregated.

—1962———1963———1964—

September 29—
Federal troops help integrate University of Mississippi ("Ole Miss") after two people are killed and several are injured.

April to May—
Birmingham, Alabama, demonstrations. School children join the marches.

May 20—
Supreme Court rules Birmingham's segregation laws are unconstitutional.

June 12—
NAACP worker Medgar Evers is killed in Jackson, Mississippi.

August 28—
March on Washington draws more than 250,000 people.

September 15—
Four girls are killed when a Birmingham church is bombed.

November 22—
President John F. Kennedy is killed in Dallas, Texas.

March–June—
St. Augustine, Florida, demonstrations.

June 21—
James Chaney, Michael Schwerner, and Andrew Goodman are killed while registering black voters in Mississippi.

July 2—
Civil Rights Act is passed. Among other things, it provides for equal job opportunities and gives the government power to sue to desegregate public schools and facilities.

August—
Mississippi Freedom Democratic Party (MFDP) attempts to represent Mississippi at the Democratic National Convention.

—1958———1959————1960————1961—

September 1958–August 1959—
Little Rock Central High School is closed because governor refuses to integrate it.

February 1—
Student sit-ins at lunch counter in Greensboro, North Carolina, begin sit-in protests all over the South.

April 17—
Student Nonviolent Coordinating Committee (SNCC) is founded.

May 6—
Civil Rights Act is passed. Among other things, it allows judges to appoint people to help blacks register to vote.

Eleven African countries win their independence.

May 4—
Freedom Rides leave Washington, D.C., and head south.

September 22—
Interstate Commerce Commission ordered to enforce desegregation laws on buses, and trains, and in travel facilities like waiting rooms, rest rooms, and restaurants.

—1965———1966————1967————1968—

January–March—
Selma, Alabama, demonstrations.

February 21—
Malcolm X is killed in New York City.

March 21–25—
More than 25,000 march from Selma to Montgomery, Alabama.

August 6—
Voting Rights Act passed.

August 11–16—
Watts riot (Los Angeles, California).

June—
James Meredith "March Against Fear" from Memphis, Tennessee, to Jackson, Mississippi. Stokely Carmichael makes slogan "Black Power" famous during march.

Fall—
Black Panther Party for Self-Defense is formed by Huey Newton and Bobby Seale in Oakland, California.

June 13—
Thurgood Marshall is appointed first African-American U.S. Supreme Court justice.

Summer—
Riots break out in 30 U.S. cities.

April 4—
Martin Luther King, Jr., is killed in Memphis, Tennessee.

April 11—
Civil Rights Act is passed. Among other things, it prohibits discrimination in selling and renting houses or apartments.

May 13–June 23—
Poor People's March: Washington, D.C., to protest poverty.

CIVIL RIGHTS MOVEMENT TIME LINE　**3**

1 THEY CALLED HER FUNDI

> *Ella Jo Baker, one of the key persons in the formation of SNCC [the Student Nonviolent Coordinating Committee], is one of those many strong black women who have devoted their lives to the liberation of their people. She has an endless faith in people and their power to change their status in life.*
>
> *She believes strongly in the organized will of the people as opposed to the power of a single leader. She has served black people without fanfare, publicity, or concern for personal credit.*
>
> **James Forman,** *The Making of Black Revolutionaries*

Ella Baker said that when she was a little girl she was bossy. She got a kick out of taking charge and telling other kids what to do. As she grew up, her bossiness developed into an outstanding ability to organize. She was able to bring people together and inspire them to work for the things that would make their lives better.

For Ella Baker, organizing was more than a job. What she did came from her heart and soul. She had a deep desire to help people in need, and that is what she spent most of her life doing. One of her greatest achievements was organizing African Americans in their fight for freedom. Her goal was to free her people from racial prejudice and discrimination. Blacks in the United States have struggled for centuries to remove these injustices. The civil rights movement that erupted in 1955 gave this struggle more power than it had ever had. Ella Baker played a major role in that movement.

Ella Baker stood barely an inch above five feet. She had a slim figure, and her brown skin was more dark than light. When she talked to you face-to-face, she kept her voice soft and low. But when she spoke in front of a group of people, her voice boomed out powerfully and dramatically.

Ella Baker had strong opinions and never backed away from saying what she thought. She was independent and followed her own thinking. She could not be pressured into doing anything that she believed wasn't right. Her directness and independence made some people feel that she was hard to get along with. But her directness and independence reflected her honesty. Most of the people who knew Ella Baker understood this, and they loved and admired her for these qualities.

The writer Howard Zinn took part in the civil rights movement. In one of his books Zinn described Ella Baker as "the most tireless, the most modest, and the wisest activist I [knew] in the struggle for human rights." An activist is someone who becomes a dedicated worker for a cause. As an activist, Ella Baker never seemed to run out of the energy or the wisdom she needed to get things done. Howard Zinn was right when he said Baker was modest. In spite of her achievements, she never considered herself to be important. She had no desire to be written up in the newspapers or to appear on TV. She had no interest in receiving public attention of any kind. She preferred to work behind the scenes, letting others take full credit for whatever was accomplished.

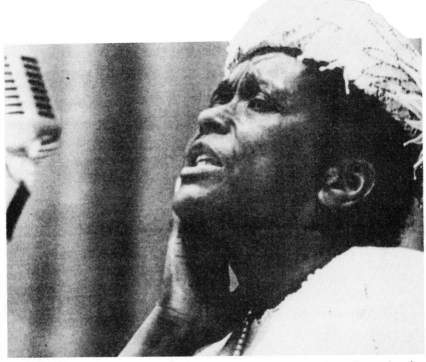

Ella Baker became a powerful, impassioned speaker for the civil rights movement.

A young woman who heard Ella Baker speak at a banquet wanted to meet her. When the banquet ended, she went up to Baker and began to introduce herself by saying, "I'm nobody..." Before the woman could get another word out, Ella Baker said, "Be quiet, child, everybody's somebody. Just be sure that when you walk, take deep, strong steps so the children coming behind you know where to go."

That incident shows two things about the way Ella Baker thought and worked. First, she believed that everybody has something to contribute. She also believed that what each of us learns must be passed on to others. In that way, the move toward a goal continues to go forward.

There is a film about Ella Baker called *Fundi*. The word *fundi* comes from Swahili, one of the many languages spoken in Africa. It is the name given to someone who generously and unselfishly shares his or her knowledge and skills with others. When you read Ella Baker's story, you will understand why she is called Fundi.

 **FAMILY TREE**

> *❝ ...one may get the idea that some of the slaves did not want freedom. This is not true. I have never seen one who did not want to be free, or one who would return to slavery. ❞*
>
> **BOOKER T. WASHINGTON,**
> *Up From Slavery*

On December 13, 1903, Georgianna and Blake Baker became the parents of a daughter whom they named Ella. She was their second child. They already had a son, Curtis. Within a few years, Curtis and Ella would have a younger sister, Margaret.

Ella Baker was born into a world that was very different from the one in which we now live. Only four days after her birth, Orville and Wilbur Wright successfully flew the world's first airplane. There were cars and trains, but most people still traveled by horse and buggy. The same year, the first full-length movie came out. It was a silent western called *The Great Train Robbery*. Many things that we now take for granted—including TV and radio—would not be invented for many years.

All three of the Baker children had been born in Norfolk, Virginia. Their mother, however, did not like Norfolk's humid weather. So, the family moved to Littleton, North Carolina, when Ella was eight years old.

Ella spent her childhood in a part of the country where racial prejudice and discrimination were particularly harsh. Both Norfolk and Littleton were located in southern states that had Jim Crow laws.

No one knows for sure where the name Jim Crow came from. It may have come from a make-believe black character called Jim Crow. The character first appeared in minstrel shows in the 1800s. Jim Crow was supposed to be a black man, but the part was played by white men who painted their faces black. The Jim Crow character made fun of black people. White audiences roared with laughter when Mr. Jim Crow portrayed blacks as lazy, stupid, and less human than whites.

Jim Crow laws began to appear in the North during the early part of the 1800s. By the end of the Civil War in 1865, these laws had also sprung up in the South. By 1900, every southern state had a long list of Jim Crow laws. The laws may have been slightly different from one state to another, but all of them kept blacks apart from whites. Because of Jim Crow laws, blacks and whites could not live in the same neighborhoods. Black and white children went to separate schools. In many instances, blacks could not use public libraries or parks. Never were they allowed to swim in pools or at beaches with whites. In department stores, blacks could not try on clothing before buying. Restaurants that served whites would not serve blacks.

All over the South, there were signs on which were printed either the word *White* or the word *Colored*. (*Colored* or *Negro* was what blacks were called then. It was not until the 1960s that the people in the United States whose ancestors had been brought from Africa chose to call themselves *black* and *Afro-American*. Later they also began to use the term *African American*.) The signs hung over doorways to separate waiting rooms in bus and train stations. They were placed at separate water fountains in public buildings such as courthouses and police stations. They even marked off separate areas in cemeteries. Blacks who were caught using something that had been marked for use by whites only could be thrown into jail, beaten, or worse.

Having grown up in the South, Ella Baker certainly saw those signs and was forced to live a very segregated, or separate, life because of them. But none of this ever made her feel inferior. In fact, when Ella was six years old and still living in Norfolk, she slapped a white boy for calling her a "nigger." She knew, even at the age of six, that nigger was the most insulting thing a black could be called. At that time, it was dangerous for any black person to do what Ella did. Being a child, however, she probably never thought about playing it safe. She simply re-acted naturally and freely to the kind of name-calling that robs African Americans of their dignity and respect.

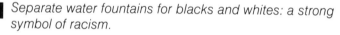
Separate water fountains for blacks and whites: a strong symbol of racism.

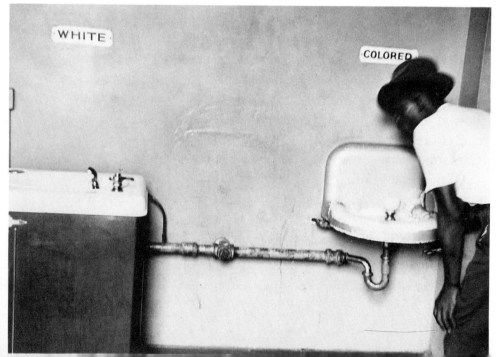

The spirit and courage Ella Baker showed that day were part of her family history. Her grandmother Betsy had suffered through an extreme form of racial prejudice and discrimination—slavery.

As a slave on a large North Carolina plantation, Betsy worked in the house of the plantation owner. House slaves cooked, cleaned, did the laundry, made clothes, and took care of the plantation owner's children. They did whatever was needed to keep the house running smoothly. As a result, house slaves had little privacy and could be awakened at any time of the night to take care of the owner's needs or wants. Still, they were often considered to be better off than the field slaves. Field slaves were the farmers on the plantation. Their work was back-breaking. These men, women, and children had to stay bent-over under the hot sun for hours while planting or picking cotton and other crops.

When Betsy reached marrying age, the plantation owner chose another house slave to be her husband. Betsy refused, showing that she had a strong, independent mind of her own. To punish Betsy, the owner made her leave the house and become a field slave. While working in the fields, she met another slave, Matthew Ross, who eventually became her husband.

When the federal government ended slavery, Matthew Ross did something remarkable. He bought several acres of land that had been part of the plantation. Matthew and Betsy lived together on the land and farmed it. Since Ross was a minister, he also built a church just a few feet away from his farm home. Today no one in Ella Baker's family knows how he was able to buy land because slaves had no money. Neither do they know how he became a minister. As a slave, Ross couldn't have gone to school for instruction in religion. In some southern states, however, slaves were allowed to sit in special sections of white churches. Sometimes plantation owners even encouraged their slaves to form their own churches. It is possible that Ross learned to become a preacher by going to a white church or having a church of his own while he was a slave on the plantation.

Ross is known to have read the Bible during his church services. This was another unusual accomplishment for a former field slave. In most of the states in which slavery existed, it was against the law to teach slaves to read and write. A number of slave owners, however, ignored those laws and taught their house slaves these skills. In other cases, slaves secretly learned to read and write without their owners' knowledge. It is possible that Betsy had been taught to read and write when she was a house slave, and later shared what she had learned with her husband.

Matthew and Betsy Ross had three daughters, one of whom was Ella Baker's mother, Georgianna. Like her parents, Georgianna had grit and determination. She became a teacher. She didn't have a college education, but she did know how to read

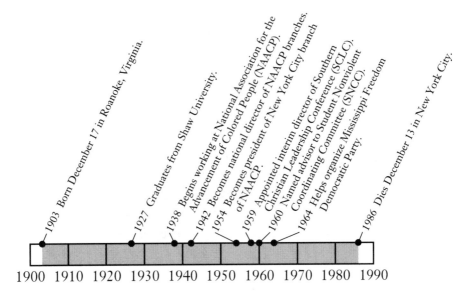

1903 Born December 17 in Roanoke, Virginia.

1927 Graduates from Shaw University.

1938 Begins working at National Association for the Advancement of Colored People (NAACP).

1942 Becomes national director of NAACP branches.

1954 Becomes president of New York City branch of NAACP.

1959 Appointed interim director of Southern Christian Leadership Conference (SCLC).

1960 Named advisor to Student Nonviolent Coordinating Committee (SNCC).

1964 Helps organize Mississippi Freedom Democratic Party.

1986 Dies December 13 in New York City.

1900 1910 1920 1930 1940 1950 1960 1970 1980 1990

and write. At that time, these skills were all a black person in the South needed in order to become a teacher. In those days, few southern schools for black children had college-trained instructors.

Georgianna was probably taught by her mother, Betsy. Also, there may have been a school in her father's church that she attended. Throughout the South, schools were often set up in black churches. These schools were run by former slaves who had learned to read and write.

Ella Baker's father, Blake Baker, was a waiter on a ferryboat. The ferry sailed from Norfolk, Virginia, to Washington, D.C., crossing the Chesapeake Bay and the Potomac River. At that time, the fastest way to travel between these two cities was by boat. There were no bridges over the two bodies of water between Norfolk and the District of Columbia.

When the family moved to North Carolina, Ella's father remained in Norfolk to keep his job on the ferryboat. Blake Baker had no skills as a farmer, and farming was the only way in which he could have made a living in the area of North Carolina where his family had settled. He wrote to his wife and children often, but he was only able to see them three or four times a year. Littleton is 150 miles from Norfolk. By horse and buggy, the cheapest way of traveling then, it took several days to go from Norfolk to Littleton.

Although Ella was far from wealthy, she had a rich heritage. The members of her family had begun their lives in the United States as slaves. Their strength of character was passed down through the generations. As a young girl, Ella learned the qualities that had enabled her family to survive: courage, ambition, the ability and desire to work hard, and a love of education. These qualities would always stay with her—and she would need them in the extraordinary life that was ahead of her.

THE ROOTS OF CARING

❝ We had a big garden, much too big for the size of the family. I'd pick a bushel or more [of fruits and vegetables], and we didn't need them, so you'd give them to the neighbors who didn't have them. That's the way you did it. It was no hassle about it. ❞

ELLA BAKER

In North Carolina, Ella Baker lived in a community that taught her to care for other people. Most of her neighbors were farmers who came from slave backgrounds. Unlike most former slaves in the South, however, these African Americans owned their own farms.

Most freed slaves did not have the money to buy land. If they wanted to be farmers, they became either tenant farmers or sharecroppers. (There were also many poor white tenant farmers and sharecroppers.) Both the tenant farmer and the sharecropper farmed on someone else's land.

Sharecroppers worked for the landowner in exchange for a share of the crops they grew. They provided the labor, and the landowner usually provided everything else—seed, tools, a horse or mule to pull the plow, and a place in which to live. Tenant farmers, however, rented the land and paid the landowner with some of the crops they grew. They needed only the land, a place in which to live, and perhaps fuel with which to cook and keep warm. They supplied their own tools, seed, and animals for plowing.

In most cases, tenant farmers gave the landowner one-third of their crop if it was corn and one-fourth if it was cotton. The landowner usually received one-half of all crops grown by the sharecroppers. For both tenant farmers and sharecroppers, no actual payments were made until the crops had been picked and sold. Tenant farmers could earn more money than sharecroppers did because they owned a larger share of the crop. But neither kind of farmer earned very much money, and there were two reasons for this.

First, the tenant farmer and the sharecropper usually bought their food, clothing, and other necessities at a store that belonged to the landowner. The advantage of this was that they could buy on credit. That meant they didn't have to pay for anything until the end of the year, after their crops had been sold. The disadvantage was that things in the landowner's store cost twice as much as in other stores.

Second, the landowner was the one who usually sold what the sharecropper and the tenant farmer planted. After the sale, the landowner then took his share of the money that was made from the crops. From the share of the money that belonged to the tenant farmer or the sharecropper, the landowner subtracted the costs of the food, clothing, and other goods that had been bought on credit. By the time this was done, many tenant farmers and sharecroppers ended up with either very little money or no money at all. Often they even found that they still owed money to the landowner.

It became a sad joke across the South that no matter how hard farmers had worked, at the end of the year the money they earned always seemed to equal what they owed the landowner. This often happened because a number of landowners weren't honest. The people who bought the crops provided a price list to show how much they would pay. This price list appeared in newspapers or was tacked up on buildings in town. After selling the crops, the landowner got a sales slip. Both the price list and the sales slip showed exactly how much money had been paid for the crops, but many tenant farmers and sharecroppers couldn't read them. They had to depend on the landowner to be honest about how much they had earned and what they owed. Because of this, the farmers and sharecroppers were easily cheated.

The end of slavery didn't put an end to the hard work that farming required. This work was the same for tenant farmers, sharecroppers, and those who farmed their own land. Tenant farmers and sharecroppers, however, were never in danger of losing their land because it didn't belong to them. But for the black landowning farmers with whom Ella Baker grew up, this was a very real danger. Crops were always threatened by such things as too much or too little rain, plant-eating bugs, or weeds. Without a good crop to sell, these farmers would have no money and might be forced to sell their land.

Fortunately, the farmers Ella Baker knew never had to lose their land. A large part of their success was due to something they had carried over from their years as slaves. Ella's grandparents told her a lot about slavery. One of the most important things they told her was how much slaves had to depend on one another in order to survive. Depending on one another meant helping and sharing in any way they could. As free blacks, the Baker family and their neighbors helped one another by sharing farm equipment, food, and money. Here's how Ella Baker described the feeling that allowed them to do this:

> There was a deep sense of community.... It wasn't a town. It was just people. And each of them had their 20-,

30-, 40-, 50-acre farms, and if there were emergencies, the farmer next to you would share in something to meet that emergency. For instance, when you thresh wheat [separate the grain from the rest of the wheat plant], if there was a [threshing machine] around, you didn't have each having his own. So you came to my farm and threshed, then you went to the next one and the next and the next one.

It is said that Ella's Grandfather Ross would borrow money to help people who were facing hard times. True to the family spirit, he did this at great personal risk. If he had failed to pay back the money, the bank that lent it to him would have taken his farm.

When she grew up, Ella Baker often told a story about the garden where the family grew their vegetables and fruits: "We had a big garden, much too big for the size of the family. I'd pick a bushel or more [of fruit or vegetables], and we didn't need them, so you'd give them to the neighbors who didn't have them. That's the way you did. It was no hassle about it."

The Baker family also shared with people who didn't live in their community. "Many a night...I have gotten up in the middle of the night when somebody knocked at the door," Ella recalled. "The train had brought somebody who was coming in either to a marriage or funeral....The first thing...you would ask if they wanted to eat something. If necessary, we'd get up and make a fire and heat up the food that was left over. Whatever was necessary to make people comfortable."

Even as a young girl, Ella Baker was busy taking care of others:

> I remember we rented some land after we moved to North Carolina. And the farmer who was living there had lots of children....And his wife died. And so the little ones would be very unkempt, and part of my weekend pleasures was to go over with clean clothes and try to catch the young ones and give 'em a bath. Being the nonfearing type...I

was 10 or 12 at the time. So you see, I'd tackle them. . . . The kids for the devilment would take off across the field. We'd chase them down, and bring them back, and put 'em in the tub, and wash 'em off, and change clothes, and carry the dirty ones home, and wash them. Those kind of things were routine.

Besides being a teacher, her mother nursed the sick in the area. One of Ella's aunts had 13 children of her own. But that didn't stop her from raising two other boys whose parents were unable to take care of them.

Ella's family and neighbors planted in her the roots of her belief in the value of sharing and caring deeply about others. That belief became the most important force in her life. Caring was "no hassle." It was "routine." Sharing was as natural as breathing. It was by caring about others and sharing her knowledge that Ella Baker achieved so much as an adult.

SCHOOL DAYS

> ❝ *I have learned that success is to be measured not so much by the position that one has reached in life as by the obstacles...overcome while trying to succeed.* ❞
>
> **BOOKER T. WASHINGTON,**
> *Up From Slavery*

Ella Baker began her study of the three Rs (reading, 'riting, and 'rithmetic) at a small public school for black children in Littleton, North Carolina. Curtis and Margaret also attended the same school. All three children were good students. Georgianna Baker not only encouraged her children to do well in school, she insisted on it. Mrs. Baker firmly believed that education was the best way to prepare a person to live a worthwhile life.

The Baker children were fortunate in being able to go to school. Getting an education was often difficult for many black children who grew up in the farm areas of the South. Some lived in places that had no schools for black youngsters. Others dropped out of school after the third or fourth grade because they had to help their parents with the farm work.

While school was in session, the Baker children had little time for play. There was homework to be done, and their mother saw to it that they did more than they had to do. If they

began to poke each other or giggle while they were supposed to be studying, Mrs. Baker always told them that their home "was a work house, not a play house."

Georgianna Baker eventually realized that her children weren't being taught well at Littleton's public school. She decided to send them to boarding school for the 9th through the 12th grades. To make up for the poor education they had received in the public school, Mrs. Baker had her children study an extra year to earn their high-school diplomas.

Each of the children was sent to a different boarding school. Ella went to Shaw University in Raleigh, North Carolina. Shaw was founded in 1865 by northern members of the American Baptist Home Mission. It is one of the oldest schools for blacks in the South. Ella enrolled in 1918, just before her 15th birthday. When she attended Shaw, it was both a high school and a university. After completing her high-school courses, she became a college student there.

At Shaw, Ella's high-school fees for classes, food, room, and books came to about $60 a year. Her college fees were higher—about $250 for the school year. Both amounts were large sums of money in those days, particularly for an African-American family. To the Bakers, that $250 was as hard to earn as $2,000 would be today.

Most of the money needed for the education of the three Baker children came from their father's earnings as a ferryboat waiter. But he wasn't able to cover the entire cost, so the children made up the difference with money they earned. Ella found jobs at Shaw during the school year, and during the summer she worked in a restaurant near Littleton. Remembering this experience, she said: "In school, I waited tables...and that provided a certain amount of money to help pay tuition, because my parents had three children in boarding school at the same time and no real money. The summer after school, I worked in a hotel....A rich lady had this place, and she decided I was to be the one to wait on her table."

The chance to wait on the owner's table might have made another person think that she was better than the other employees, but not Ella: "If I were...the head waitress, I didn't find it necessary to lord it over the man who washed dishes in the kitchen. Somewhere down the line I had a deep sense of my being part of humanity, and this I've always tried to preserve." In saying she was a "part of humanity," Ella Baker was saying that she felt a closeness with all people. She deeply believed that no one was more important than anyone else—that all people are equal.

Ella had another job to help her with the costs of school. She loved science and received excellent grades in biology and chemistry. This led a teacher to hire her to help him in the chemistry laboratory. As a lab assistant, she helped other students set up and perform experiments.

Shaw University was a Baptist school, and it was very strict. Ella and the rest of the students were given a list of rules and regulations to follow. One of them read: "No young man shall be allowed to [talk] or in any way communicate with any young lady...with the exception of the first 15 minutes after school when the young ladies and young gentlemen will be allowed to [talk] with each other."

Ella wasn't happy with many of the restrictions Shaw placed on its students. One rule in particular brought out her activist spirit. It was the rule that prevented male and female students from walking together across university grounds. She felt the rule should be removed, and other students felt the same way. With their support, Ella wrote a letter to Shaw officials asking that the rule be dropped. Ella later met with school officials and succeeded in getting the rule removed from the list of regulations

When Ella entered Shaw, she had hoped to become a medical missionary. This work would have combined her fondness for science with her desire to help people. However, this wasn't possible because a medical education was simply too expensive.

She then thought about becoming a social worker—someone who is trained to take care of the needs of others. But she found that she couldn't afford this either.

In 1927, Ella Baker graduated from Shaw University as the top student in her class. She wasn't able to do either of the things she really wanted to do, so she packed her college degree in her suitcase and left for New York City to look for work.

GONE NORTH

I, too, sing America.
I am the darker brother.
They send me
To eat in the kitchen
When company comes,
But I laugh,
And eat well,
And grow strong.
Tomorrow,
I'll be at the table
When company comes.

LANGSTON HUGHES

For several years after she arrived in New York, Ella Baker lived with relatives in a part of the city known as Harlem. For the most part, only African Americans lived in Harlem. Like Ella, many of them had migrated from the South hoping to find work. African Americans also went to New York and other northern cities for another reason: to escape the racial prejudice that was such a part of life in the South. New York wasn't free of prejudice, but things weren't as bad there as they were in the South.

Another reason Ella chose to live in New York was to avoid becoming a teacher. In the South, an educated black woman was usually expected to teach school. But Ella didn't like doing what others expected her to do.

Ella soon discovered that most educated black women in the North also became teachers. All the same, she believed that the North would offer her the opportunity to do something else with her college degree. She was going to be a pioneer. She would use her learning in ways that were seldom tried by educated black women of her generation. But she had no clear idea of what she wanted to do. Until she could find work that truly interested her, Ella did what she had done at Shaw. She took a job as a waitress in a restaurant. Later she became a factory worker.

Ella also wrote articles for Harlem newspapers. White newspapers in New York rarely carried stories about blacks. The stories they did print told only about crimes and other wrongdoings committed by blacks. Newspapers published in Harlem, however, gave a more complete picture of the lives of black people in New York and the entire United States.

One of the Harlem newspapers for which Ella wrote was called the *West Indian Review.* This paper published news about people from the West Indies, a group of islands in the Caribbean Sea. The articles were about West Indians who lived in New York and about events that took place on the islands. The *Review*'s readers were primarily blacks who had come to Harlem from such islands as Jamaica, Barbados, Trinidad-Tobago, Grenada, and Antigua. As was true of southern blacks, it was the hope of finding work that brought West Indians to New York.

When Ella Baker arrived in Harlem in 1927, the Harlem Renaissance was in full swing. The Harlem Renaissance marked a time of great artistic achievement among blacks. There were the poets Countee Cullen and Langston Hughes. Jean Toomer was writing his famous book *Cane.* Novels were also being written by Zora Neale Hurston, Wallace Thurman, Charles W. Chesnutt, Jessie Fauset, and Claude McKay, a West

The Harlem Renaissance

arlem, New York, was the center of a great creative movement among African Americans after World War I. Writers, artists, and musicians came to Harlem. It was a place where they were free to develop their crafts. Among them were writers Langston Hughes, Zora Neale Hurston, and W. E. B. Du Bois. Hughes summed up the movement when he said, "We younger Negro artists who create now intend to express to our individual dark skinned selves without fear or shame. If white people are pleased, we are glad. If they are not, it doesn't matter. We know we are beautiful. And ugly too. The tom-tom cries and the tom-tom laughs. If colored people are pleased we are glad. If they are not, their displeasure doesn't matter either. We build our temples for tomorrow, strong as we know how, and we stand on top of the mountain, free within ourselves."

Zora Neale
Hurston

Langston
Hughes

The famed Cotton Club was a showcase for black talent in Harlem.

Indian from Jamaica. The sculptor Augusta Savage was creating beautiful and powerful black bodies out of stone and metal. Hale Woodruff was painting scenes of black life.

Many other writers, poets, and artists also contributed to the spirited energy of the Harlem Renaissance. They all produced works that focused on black people's African heritage and on their pride in being black. The creative outpouring was a way of telling the people of the United States that blacks were not inferior, as many whites believed. The writing, art, and music of African Americans made a statement that they were as talented and intelligent as any other race of people.

Black scholar Alain Locke has written about some of the reasons for the birth of the Harlem Renaissance. In his book *The New Negro*, Locke said that blacks who had come up from the South were greatly changed by their experiences in northern cities. They met more people with different ideas about equality and justice than they would ever have met in southern towns. In the North there was a difference in life-style, and more economic freedom. They no longer lived in one-room wooden shacks or farmed the land. They now lived in large apartment buildings and worked in factories.

There was still prejudice against blacks in the North, but they could do things—such as vote—that they had never been able to do. In the North, blacks felt freer than they did in the South to speak out against racial prejudice and discrimination. The "new Negro" demanded that American democracy be made to work for blacks as well as it did for whites. This demand is what the black writers and artists of the Harlem Renaissance expressed in their works.

At this time, Harlem was alive with ideas for changing the way things were. Marcus Garvey, who came from Jamaica, spread the idea that blacks had no future in the United States. He said the only place in which blacks could be completely free was Africa. He suggested that blacks go back to Africa. Throughout the country, thousands of blacks were willing to do just that. But Garvey's back-to-Africa movement was stopped when the U.S. government accused him of cheating his followers out of millions of dollars they had donated. There were many people who believed that the government's accusation wasn't true. Nevertheless, Marcus Garvey was arrested and ordered to return to Jamaica.

During this time, blacks also discussed other ideas about the way in which governments were run and the type of government that would be best for them. For example, would blacks receive better treatment under a Communist government, a Socialist government, or a capitalist government? Some people favored communism. They argued that in a Communist country, blacks would no longer have to live in poverty and face discrimination. The idea behind communism is that everyone is equal. In a Communist society, there are supposedly no rich or poor, no important and unimportant people. According to Communist belief, the people should own all industry and businesses, and the people are supposed to share equally in everything.

The argument in favor of socialism was very much like the one in favor of communism. Communism developed from socialism. There would be no rich or poor in a Socialist society. Everyone would be treated as equals. Together, the people would also own industry and business, and share the income equally. In an ideal Communist or Socialist country, everyone who could work would have a job.

The United States is a capitalist society, one in which people do not have to share what they own or earn. Ideally, there is no limit on how much wealth one person can acquire. In capitalist countries, most businesses are owned by individuals and not by the people as a whole. Businesses compete with one another, and the profits they earn are not shared equally. Owners and bosses usually make more money than ordinary workers do.

Everywhere in Harlem, there were lively debates about communism, socialism, and capitalism. People discussed the ways in which each system might be better or worse for black people. At the heart of all the talk was the question of how equality and well-being could be brought to African Americans.

Ella Baker was excited about all that she heard in Harlem and eagerly joined the discussions. She went all over Harlem and other parts of New York City to exchange ideas with other people. She recalled: "Wherever there was a discussion, I'd go. It didn't matter if it was all men, and maybe I was the only woman...it didn't matter.... New York was the hotbed of radical [extreme] thinking."

These discussions made Ella more aware that it might be possible to help a large number of people to change their lives for the better. As she learned more about the ideas of the great thinkers of her time, Ella began to develop ideas of her own. Soon she would have the chance to take some of those ideas and put them into action.

6 TEACHER, AFTER ALL

❝ The major job was getting people to understand that they had something within their power that they could use. ❞

ELLA BAKER

Life in the United States became difficult in 1929. The Great Depression started and lasted until the early 1940s. During the depression, thousands of businesses closed, and factories shut down. Millions of people lost their jobs, and those who were lucky enough to have work got paid less for it.

The weather didn't help either. In states like Oklahoma, Colorado, and Kansas, heavy winds blew continually and there was little rain. Topsoil turned to dust and blew away, making it impossible for farmers to grow crops. Many left their farms and

33

The Great Depression brought people in droves to shelters and soup kitchens like this one.

went west to California and Oregon to look for work on farms that were still able to grow crops.

All across the country there were soup kitchens that provided free food. Every day, long lines of hungry men, women, and children waited patiently for a bowl of soup and a piece of bread.

Like many other things during this time, the Harlem Renaissance came to an end in 1929. Most of the art works produced by the black painters and sculptors of the Harlem Renaissance had been bought by well-to-do whites who could no longer afford to buy works of art. Harlem Renaissance writers, too, faced the same problem. They could no longer get their books published. For the most part, their writings had been printed by white publishers. These publishers had never made much money publishing the works of black writers. If they had continued to publish black writers, they would have made even less money because people had less to spend.

Ella Baker was fortunate to have a job. During the early part of the depression, she worked in the Harlem office of a black newspaper. Having George Schuyler as a co-worker doubled her good fortune. George Schuyler was one of the leading black newspaper writers of the time. He was known as a "race man" because his newspaper articles often attacked whites for their racial prejudice. He also urged blacks to boldly fight for their rights.

One day Schuyler wrote an article in which he suggested a way of helping people who had been hurt by the depression. Many families didn't have much money and even found it difficult to buy food. Schuyler's plan would allow them to buy more with the dollars they had. It called for people to get together in groups. Each person in the group would put up a certain amount of money. Because such a group would have more money to spend than was possible for one person alone, food and other necessary items could be bought in larger quantities.

Goods purchased in large quantities cost less than those bought in small amounts. For instance, in the 1930s, a pound of potatoes might cost 10 cents, but a sack of potatoes containing five pounds might be priced at 30 cents. That meant that each pound in the sack would cost only 6 cents. Buying several five-pound sacks of potatoes could reduce the price to something like 20 cents a sack—the larger the quantity, the greater the savings. This is true even today. Also, to get the best prices, the group would not shop in supermarkets or little grocery stores. Instead, they would buy their goods from food wholesalers. (Wholesalers are dealers who sell only large amounts of any item—vegetables, fruits, or meat). After they had been purchased, the goods would be divided among group members.

The program that George Schuyler suggested is called a cooperative because the members of the group cooperate, or work together, in order to save money. Schuyler received such a good response from those who read his article on cooperatives that he decided to set one up. He asked Ella Baker to help him. Their efforts were so successful that before long they found them-selves assisting in the development of black cooperatives all over the country. George Schuyler and Ella Baker didn't form or operate these cooperatives themselves. Instead, they gave people advice on how to start them and run them.

The cooperatives reminded Ella Baker of the way of life she had known as a young girl in North Carolina. The people in cooperatives, like the farmers Ella had known as a child, real-ized the importance of sharing. They shared money, and they shared the food their money could buy. By working together, these people found that they had the power to solve a problem that was common to all of them. One person acting alone could never have such power.

George Schuyler and Ella Baker began the cooperatives proj-ect in 1932. Within three years, Ella Baker had become an expert on consumer affairs. This meant that she could teach people how to buy quality food and other items for less money. She was so good at shopping that she was hired by the Works Progress Administration (WPA) to help others who had been hurt by the depression.

The WPA was part of a group of programs that had been established by President Franklin D. Roosevelt beginning in 1933 . These programs were developed to bring the country out of the Great Depression and were called the New Deal. By 1935, the year the WPA was formed, the depression had been going on for six years. One of the major goals of Roosevelt's programs was to help the millions of Americans who still had no jobs. The main purpose of the WPA was to give people work for which the federal government paid them.

The WPA and other New Deal work programs, such as the Civil Works Administration and the Civilian Conservation Corps (CCC), employed a large number of people. Under the CCC, millions of young people planted 10 million trees and repaired bridges and roads across the country. Work on new bridges, roads, and buildings got started as well. Some of the

largest dams in the United States were begun under New Deal programs. These include the Grand Coulee Dam in the state of Washington, Boulder Dam on the Colorado River, and the dams built on the Tennessee River by the Tennessee Valley Authority. These dams help to control the flow of water on farmlands and provide cities and towns with electricity.

People with artistic skills also found work in WPA projects. Painters created murals for the walls of schools, hospitals, and libraries. Sculptors made statues for parks and other outdoor areas. Teams of writers were assigned to each state to write a history of that state. A group of black writers wrote about the history of blacks in the city of New York.

In addition, WPA workers were employed in community projects that provided free services. Some of these projects were art and dance classes, sewing classes, reading classes for adults, and classes for sports. Ella Baker worked in a WPA community project in Harlem. As a shopping expert, it was her job to provide advice on buying. More and more people were going back to work, but most of them weren't earning large salaries. Ella Baker's buying classes taught people how to get the most for their money.

In describing her work with the WPA, Ella Baker said: "I was with the WPA...consumer education project. I was a teacher....In the WPA, we developed a brochure [booklet]...that raised the question of quality: why you judge the quality of goods; what you buy; where you could buy best; how best you could use your buying power....We had classes in the settlement houses [community centers] or in women's clubs or wherever else you could."

Ella Baker taught classes on buying for three years. In 1938, she left the WPA to work with one of the most important African-American organizations in the United States—the National Association for the Advancement of Colored People.

Z ON THE ROAD

In 1938, Ella Baker went to work for the oldest civil rights organization in the United States. That organization is the National Association for the Advancement of Colored People (NAACP). It was formed in 1909 by an interracial (black and white) group of men and women in New York. Here Baker would actively fight segregation and discrimination against African Americans. The NAACP was concerned about every kind of discrimination toward blacks, but in the beginning, its number-one concern was lynching. Lynching is the killing of a person—often by hanging—who is accused of a crime, without giving that person a trial.

From the 1880s to the 1930s, almost 4,500 lynchings took place in the United States. Close to 3,000 of those lynched were black. Most of the other victims were white, although some Chinese Americans and Native Americans were also lynched. Lynchings took place in both the North and the South, but there were many more of these killings in the South.

Lynchings have occurred in the United States for more than 200 years. In the southern states, the number of lynchings greatly increased after the Civil War ended in 1865. During the war, in 1863, President Abraham Lincoln outlawed slavery in the South. Many white southerners were angry because they had not only lost the war, but they had also lost their cheap labor—slaves. These whites felt that free blacks in the South had to be "kept in their place." Otherwise they would think they were as good as whites and begin competing with whites for land and jobs. Jim Crow laws helped whites to keep blacks in their place by keeping blacks separate from whites and forcing them to live in inferior conditions. Lynchings became the most cruel way of keeping blacks in their place.

Blacks were lynched for such things as talking back to a white person or having a job that was usually given only to whites. These acts were considered crimes. Often a black man was lynched if it was thought that he was having a relationship with a white woman. A black man could be lynched for no other reason than the fact that a white person pointed a finger at him and said, "He did it." The black victim was then accused of some crime, such as murder or stealing, but it often turned out that he had done nothing wrong at all.

Even if a black person had committed a crime, he or she should have had the right to a fair trial. But there were times when even the police took part in the lynchings. Even when they were not directly involved, the police often did nothing to stop the lynchings. People who took part in lynching a black person were rarely charged with committing a crime. In fact, if they went to jail at all, they were usually released without suffering any penalty. Those who were put on trial for what they had done were almost never found guilty.

One of the most famous and outrageous examples of this injustice took place nearly 100 years after the Civil War. Emmett Till, a black eighth grader from Chicago, was visiting relatives in Money, Mississippi. Emmett and his cousin Curtis Jones were passing the time at Bryant's Grocery and Meat Market with some other boys. One of them dared Emmett to go into the store and say something to Carolyn Bryant, a white woman who was inside. Emmett went in, bought some candy, and said "Bye, baby" to her as he walked out. The boys laughed, and later they all forgot about the joke.

According to later accounts, Carolyn Bryant's husband and her brother went to Curtis's house a few nights after the incident in the grocery store. They dragged 14-year-old Emmett out of the house and drove him to the side of the Tallahatchie River. They tied a 75-pound cotton-gin fan to Emmett's neck with barbed wire, stripped him, gouged out one of his eyes, then shot him in the head and dumped his body into the river. Later the two men even admitted to the killing. All the same, an all-white jury found them not guilty.

The NAACP fought to get laws passed that would prohibit lynching. The organization usually fought its battles in court. NAACP lawyers made legal cases out of situations in which blacks were discriminated against. These lawyers then argued in court to show in what way this treatment was against the law. An example of such a situation was the case against the city of Louisville, Kentucky, in 1917. Louisville had a law that prevented blacks from living wherever they wanted to live in the city. The NAACP argued against the law. In this case, the court agreed with the NAACP and ruled that the law was not legal.

In the fight against lynching, however, the NAACP chose another method. Lynchings were taking place in many states, and it would have been too expensive to have legal battles going on in each of them. Besides, the chances of winning this fight in southern states were rather slim. The NAACP therefore tried to get the United States Congress to pass a law against lynching.

A law that came from Congress would be the law in all the states. In 1922, Congress did consider making such a law. Although the law was not passed then, the debate in Congress on lynching received a lot of media attention. This attention, along with the fact that the NAACP continued to speak out against lynching, caused a big drop in the number of lynchings from that year onward.

In her first job with the NAACP, Ella Baker was an assistant field secretary. The organization had offices, called branches, in every state. Field secretaries visited these branches to raise money and find new members. These field workers played a vital part in keeping the NAACP strong and active. Without a growing number of members, the organization would not be able to claim that it spoke for all black people. Without money, it would lose its power to fight for the rights of African Americans.

As an assistant field secretary, Ella Baker was sent to NAACP banches in the South. She was on the road for about six months out of the year, sometimes traveling to a different city each day. In describing the traveling, Baker said: "I left [New York] about the 14th of February and I never came back until the end of June. I...would swing from Florida into Alabama, Georgia...all the way up into Virginia and then back; which meant that I had this very wide contact with people."

Ella Baker had lived with Jim Crow laws, and she certainly must have known about lynching when she was growing up in North Carolina. She knew how difficult it would be to get black southerners to join an organization that fought Jim Crow laws and lynchings. It would be difficult because it was dangerous, for her and for the blacks she spoke with. Many southern whites hated the NAACP. To them the organization was a troublemaker. To make matters worse, because its headquarters was in New York City, the organization was a *northern* troublemaker. It urged southern blacks to resist Jim Crow laws and demand their rights as American citizens. Many southern whites wanted nothing that would change the way of life in the South. They would do just about anything to keep the NAACP out and blacks from becoming members. In his book *An American Dilemma*, the sociologist Gunnar Myrdal recalled what a white southerner once said: "Anybody from the organization [NAACP] sneaking into the [southern] community will have to run fast in order not to get lynched."

Ella Baker may never have run for her life from a lynch mob, but there were many horror stories about other black NAACP members in the South and what happened to them. For instance, throughout the South, black teachers and principals in black schools were paid less than were white teachers and principals in white schools. In Florida, NAACP member Harry T. Moore worked on correcting this situation. In telling Moore's story, Ella Baker said: "Harry T. Moore was one of three black principals in Florida who [were] fired when they began to talk in terms of equal pay. The [difference in pay] between black and white teachers was tragic, to say the least.... I think it was Christmas Eve... dynamite was placed under his bedroom. He and his wife were blown to smithereens."

Much of the violence toward southern blacks came from such groups as the Ku Klux Klan (KKK). The KKK got started in 1865, just after the Civil War ended. It began in Tennessee, then quickly spread to other southern states. KKK members believed that whites were better than any other race. The KKK wanted to make sure that blacks would have no power. The KKK believed that only whites should govern the way things were run in the South. To accomplish this goal, the KKK prevented blacks from voting. The group also kept many blacks poor by not allowing them to get well-paying jobs.

In order to control blacks, the KKK used terror, or the threat of terror, against them. Its members usually carried on their activities at night. To keep their identities secret, they hid their heads and faces by wearing high cone-shaped hats and hoods, as well as long white robes to cover their bodies. They were a frightening sight, especially to the southern blacks who were awakened from their sleep by a visit from the KKK. Sometimes

One of the most terrifying scenes of racism: a cross-burning by the Ku Klux Klan.

the KKK just gave a warning by placing a tall wooden cross in front of a black family's house and setting the cross on fire. But more often, blacks were dragged from their homes and badly whipped or lynched.

The Ku Klux Klan died down after only a few years, but it sprang back to life again around 1915 in Georgia. From there, KKK groups began to appear in the North as well. In its second birth, the KKK spread hatred not only against blacks but also immigrants, Roman Catholics, and Jews. Its members believed that the United States of America belonged only to whites who were members of a Protestant religion.

In spite of their activities against these other groups, the Ku Klux Klan was never as violent toward Catholics and Jews as it was toward blacks. Their fear of the KKK kept many blacks in the South from demanding equal rights of any kind. That fear also prevented them from joining organizations that fought for equal rights. As part of her job, Ella Baker helped people to overcome their fear of the KKK and to find the courage to join the NAACP.

Baker felt that she could be most effective by speaking to groups rather than to one person at a time. In discussing how she operated, she said:

> Where did people gather? They gathered in churches. In schools. And you'd get permission. You'd call up Reverend so-and-so and ask if you could appear before the congregation at such-and-such a time. Sometimes they'd give you three minutes, because, after all, many people weren't secure enough to run the risk, as they saw it, of being targeted as ready to challenge the powers that be. And they'd say, "You have three minutes after the church service." And you'd take it. And you'd use it, to the extent to which you can be persuasive [convincing]. It's the ammunition you have. It's all you have.

The NAACP fought for the rights of all blacks. But for a long time after the organization began, most of its southern black members were professional men and women—doctors, teachers, business owners, and lawyers. Gunnar Myrdal believed the NAACP did this because educated people are the easiest group of people to organize.

Ella Baker, however, felt that the organization should do more to encourage ordinary workers to become members. These blacks—janitors, street cleaners, construction workers, gardeners, housekeepers, drivers, and the like—often depended on whites for their jobs. They were the ones who needed the NAACP the most. During her trips to the South, these were the people Baker tried hardest to reach. She had to help them understand that the NAACP hadn't been formed just for professional blacks.

Baker was an educated woman, but she was also down-to-earth. She could make less educated people feel that she was one of them. In an interview, she described the importance of being able to do this:

> ...[Y]our success depended on both your disposition [personality] and your capacity to sort of stimulate people— and how you carried yourself, in terms of not being above people. And see, there were more people who were not economically secure [well-off in terms of money] than there were economically secure people....I remember one place I got a contribution for a life membership in the NAACP, which was five hundred dollars then, from a longshoremen's union. They remembered somebody who had been there before from the NAACP with a mink coat. When they gave this five hundred dollar membership, somebody mentioned it. See, they had resented the mink coat. I don't think it was the mink coat that they really resented. It was the barrier they could sense between them and the person in the coat. See, you can have a mink coat on and you can identify with the man who is working on the docks....If you really identify with him, what you wear won't make a ...bit of difference. But if you talk differently, and somehow talk down to people, they can sense it. They can feel it. And they know whether you are talking *with* them, or talking *at* them, or talking *about* them.

It was clear that the people Ella Baker visited felt that she was talking *with* them, not *at* them. When she first left New York City to help recruit new members in the South, there were fewer NAACP members there than in any other part of the country. By 1941, because of Baker's efforts and those of other field workers, the number of southern NAACP members had risen greatly.

Ella Baker was an NAACP assistant field secretary for four years. In 1942, she received a promotion.

WAR, LOVE, AND SNEAKERS

> *66 ...work is not simply the output of energy, nor the functioning of certain muscles ... people work more by using their brains and their hearts. 99*

FRANTZ FANON, *The Wretched of the Earth*

I n 1942, Ella Baker became the director of branches for the NAACP. She was now responsible for managing the activities of all the local branches in cities and towns across the United States. As director, Baker helped branches organize drives to increase membership and raise funds. She encouraged branches to become involved in solving the problems of black communities. She also provided instruction in handling these problems.

For example, there might be a need for a traffic light in an area in which blacks lived. Ella Baker would advise the branch on how to present the case to city officials. Sometimes a petition—a written statement signed by a large number of people asking that something be done—was needed. Baker would help to prepare one that would have the greatest effect on the problem.

It would have been just about impossible for the NAACP to function without its branches. In addition to providing the organization with members and money, the branches also kept NAACP headquarters in touch with what was happening to blacks throughout the country. Knowing what was going on in branch locations was extremely important to the NAACP because of the way it operated. Its main job was to fight for the equal rights of blacks in the courts—in local, state, and federal courts of law. In its legal battles, the NAACP argued that racial segregation and discrimination went against the Constitution of the United States—particularly the 14th and 15th Amendments.

The 14th Amendment was added to the U.S. Constitution in 1868, three years after the Civil War ended. As a result of this amendment, blacks who had once been slaves became citizens of the United States. Naturally, this meant that former slaves should have the same rights as other citizens. The Constitution granted citizenship to all people who were born in the United States and made it illegal for any state law to take away these rights. The 15th Amendment was added to the U.S. Constitution in 1870. This amendment protects the right to vote. It states that the right to vote cannot be denied to any U.S. citizen because of race or color, or for having been a slave. Since blacks were made citizens under the 14th Amendment, this amendment protected the right of black males to vote. (Women—black and white—did not gain the right to vote until 1920.)

The branches provided the NAACP's national office with cases that could be taken to court. Through its branches, NAACP headquarters learned of attempts in several states to prevent blacks from entering universities to study for professional degrees.

The NAACP was especially interested in increasing educational opportunities for African Americans. At that time not many blacks could get beyond the four-year college degree. Without further education, African Americans couldn't work in such professions as medicine and law. Few black colleges and universities provided that kind of instruction, and most white medical schools and law schools refused to accept black students. From the 1930s through the 1950s, the NAACP fought and won court battles to have blacks admitted to schools in Maryland, Texas, Missouri, and Oklahoma.

In 1939, World War II broke out in Europe. The United States entered the war two years later, when the Japanese bombed the American naval base at Pearl Harbor, Hawaii, on December 7, 1941. This was shortly before Ella Baker became director of branches. Fighting the war were the Allied forces (United States, Great Britain, Russia, China) on one side and the Axis powers (Germany, Italy, Japan) on the other side. The war lasted until 1945.

During the war years, the federal government called on Ella Baker to return to consumer affairs—an area in which she had become an expert at the time of the Great Depression. During the depression, the problem had been a shortage of jobs and money. During the war years, the problem was a shortage of food, shoes, gas, and many other vital products.

This shortage existed because so much of everything went to the military. Soldiers needed weapons, but they also needed food. Gas was also needed—to keep airplanes, ships, and tanks in action. As a result, many goods were in short supply for the civilians at home. Living with that shortage was considered to be part of their contribution to the war effort. Civilians were, however, given ration stamps to buy items that were scarce. This system made sure these items were equally available to everyone by controlling the amount of food or gas each civilian could buy. A stamp might, for instance, limit the purchase of sugar to two pounds a month.

At the request of the federal government, Ella Baker studied the effect of rationing on blacks in New York City, primarily in Harlem. Studies like this were being conducted on Americans across the country because the government wanted to know whether rationing was damaging people's health. Baker and a group of assistants questioned shoppers in Harlem stores. They were asked what they had bought and whether they felt they were able to buy enough food in spite of rationing. As a result of this study, Baker suggested that a ration stamp should not be limited to buying only one item. She felt that instead of having to use one stamp to buy butter, another to buy meat, and still another to buy cheese, the consumer should be able to choose— to use a stamp to buy any one of these foods. The government put her idea into operation.

Baker made the study for the government at the same time that she was carrying out her duties as an NAACP officer. In order to do both jobs, she had to work long hours every day of the week. But Ella Baker was used to working hard. The war had made life more difficult for everybody. As Ella Baker saw it, however, the war could also do some good by creating job opportunities for African Americans. Jobs in factories and plants that made war equipment were jobs that could teach new skills. These were jobs that African Americans had been pre-vented from getting.

Ella Baker was right. Many people who normally held fac-tory jobs had gone into the military, so an urgent call went out for workers to replace them. Baker urged NAACP branches to encourage blacks in their areas to answer this call. Without going into court, the organization would win an important vic-tory. Thousands of black men who were not in the armed forces because of age or physical disability were able to find work. With their new experience, these workers would learn valuable skills that could help them win jobs after the war as well.

Women—both black and white—found work, too. The de-mand for workers was so great that more women than ever before became job holders—and they were doing what men usually did. They hammered, welded, drilled, and riveted as they put together destroyers, bombers, submarines, and other machines of war. They even had their own symbol. It was a female cartoon character known as Rosie the Riveter. Rosie was dressed in overalls and held a riveting gun in her hand. Paintings of Rosie appeared on posters issued by the government, encouraging women to support the war effort.

An African-American woman does her part in the nation's defense effort during World War II.

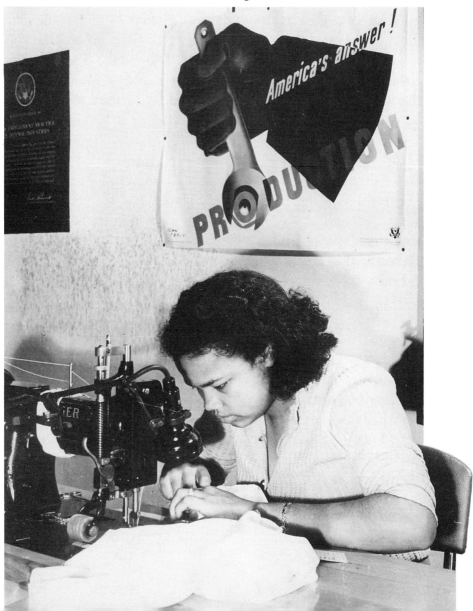

Ella Baker was still doing a great deal of traveling for the NAACP, visiting the various branches and meeting with branch members. But in 1946, she felt that she could no longer be away from home for long periods of time. There was something else in her life that needed her full attention. Baker resigned from the NAACP to take care of her niece, Jackie.

Jackie had been living in Littleton where Baker herself grew up. When Jackie was eight years old, her aunt brought her to New York. According to Jackie, Aunt Ella did this because "she thought that every child should have the opportunity to grow up with someone who loved them and someone who could care for them. And she felt she could give me that." When she was asked whether Aunt Ella was strict, Jackie said: "She was very firm, but she would never say you could not do something and that's it. She always thought you should have an explanation. You knew that the love was there and there wasn't anything she wouldn't do for you."

Jackie lived with her aunt in an apartment in Harlem. Ella Baker devoted herself to making sure that her niece got used to her new home and neighborhood. Jackie had to be enrolled in school, signed up for summer camp, and introduced to activities and people in her new surroundings. But a woman like Baker couldn't stay away from work that involved helping people.

Within a year after leaving the NAACP, Baker set up Harlem's first office of the American Cancer Society. It provided information on how to reduce the possibility of getting cancer and how to recognize signs of the disease. She also became involved in other efforts to help the black community. Most of Harlem's blacks were now earning a better living than they had during the 1930s. Some of them were even quite well-off. However, Baker was concerned about the poor, and she took part in community projects to find jobs and better housing for them.

To Ella Baker, a job wasn't just what you did in order to make money. As Jackie learned, it was any responsibility you had for doing something. Remembering life with her aunt, Jackie said: "Aunt Ella used to say that everybody had a job. I remember when I was in school, my job was to go to school and do my best. Her job was to take care of me and to make sure that I had food, clothing, and everything else I needed."

One of Jackie's most vivid memories of her aunt had to do with a pair of sneakers:

> On one occasion, I wanted sneakers. But I didn't really need them. I had shoes. There was a little boy next door who took a liking to my aunt. He was beginning to play basketball with the other boys. He had no shoes at all and he wanted sneakers, too. So we decided we would buy him sneakers, and I could wait for another time to buy sneakers for me. We decided on that because Aunt Ella felt that his self-image had been destroyed because he did not have the proper attire [clothing] to play in. And we could sacrifice my sneakers for his at this point if it helped him in any way. If he began to feel good about himself, then it was worth it. That was the type of thing she would do for people.

With the same love and care that she answered a child's need for a pair of sneakers, Ella Baker later became involved in every child's need for a good education.

MADAM PRESIDENT

" *I'll never rest, never as long as there is a single Negro boy or girl without the chance that every human being deserves— the chance to prove his worth.* **"**

MARY McLEOD BETHUNE,
educator

In 1954, Jackie celebrated her 16th birthday, and Aunt Ella returned to the NAACP. This time Ella Baker became the president of the New York City branch. The year would be an extraordinary one for both of them and all African Americans.

In May 1954, the Supreme Court of the United States determined that a Supreme Court decision made in 1896 had been wrong. That earlier Court told the state of Louisiana that its trains could have separate sections for black passengers and white passengers. That was all right, the Court had said, as long as both the black and the white sections were equal in quality and comfort.

The 1896 case that the Supreme Court ruled on was known as *Plessy v. Ferguson*. The idea of "separate but equal" had spread from Louisiana to all the other southern states and to some northern states as well. It had become the legal basis of all the Jim Crow laws that placed black and white children in separate, or segregated, schools. It had blacks and whites sitting in separate waiting rooms in bus, train, and plane terminals. In general, this idea separated whites and blacks from each other as much as possible, particularly in the South.

Being kept separate was insulting and humiliating to blacks. In addition, what was separate was rarely equal. Black train riders rode in cars that weren't as comfortable and clean as those for white riders. Black public schools weren't given as much money for books and equipment as were white public schools. Almost anything marked for blacks received less care and attention than things that were intended for whites.

In the early 1950s, NAACP lawyers took a case known as *Brown v. the Board of Education of Topeka, Kansas* to the Supreme Court. This case challenged the idea of "separate but equal." It was started by the Reverend Oliver Brown, who got tired of seeing his seven-year-old daughter Linda walk right past a white school in Topeka and cross dangerous railroad tracks to reach the school bus that would take her to a black school several miles from home.

Rev. Oliver Brown went to the Topeka branch of the NAACP to see whether his daughter's situation could be used to protest the "separate but equal" law. The Topeka branch agreed that a legal case could be made. A team of NAACP lawyers, led by Thurgood Marshall, argued the case before the Supreme Court. On May 17, 1954, the Supreme Court announced its decision on the case. The Court ruled that separate was not equal. This meant that it was no longer legal for black and white children to go to segregated public schools—schools that were all or mostly black, or all or mostly white.

The Supreme Court's ruling was immediately recognized as a landmark decision—one that would affect many other laws and practices throughout the United States. The NAACP now knew that it was possible to change the Supreme Court's mind about laws that discriminated against African Americans. If a law that allowed separate schools could be changed, laws that allowed separate waiting rooms, train cars, and restaurants could also be changed. Laws could be passed that would outlaw unequal pay, housing, and health care. The *Brown v. Board of Education* decision didn't just mean that Linda Brown wouldn't have to walk across railroad tracks to get to school anymore. It was a step toward equality for all African Americans in every walk of life.

The officials of New York City believed that segregated schools did not exist there. But there were other New Yorkers who had a different point of view. Ella Baker was one of them. From elementary to high school in Harlem, Jackie had been a student in classes that were almost all black. Baker and other New Yorkers began to put pressure on the city government to take a closer look at the school system.

In 1955, the mayor of New York City set up the Commission on School Integration to make a study. He asked Ella Baker to be a member of the commission. Commission members visited every school in the city and talked to students, teachers, and principals. Finally, the commission made its report in 1957. Many city officials were surprised to find out that segregation did indeed exist in many of the city's schools. The commission had discovered that some schools were mostly black and others were mostly white. A few were all white or all black.

Jim Crow laws hadn't created this segregation, as they had in the South. New York's segregation had come about because most black and white families didn't live in the same neighborhoods. Even when they did, one or the other race would be there in much larger numbers. Unlike Linda Brown, most children in New York City attended public schools that were close to their homes. So, the schools were racially like the communities in which they were located. They were mostly white or mostly black because that's the way the neighborhoods were.

Shortly after the commission's report came out, Ella Baker set up meetings around the city for parents of children in the city's public schools. In these meetings, the report was discussed. Black parents were particularly upset about one part of the report. It stated that black children who went to their neighborhood schools had lower test scores than did the children at other schools. Baker encouraged parents to send petitions to the city. In those petitions, black parents asked that their children be allowed to attend schools outside of their own neighborhoods.

The commission's report, along with the demands from parents, forced the city to develop a plan that would put an end to segregation in the schools. In 1961, the open-enrollment program was started. Open enrollment allowed elementary and high-school students to go to schools outside of their neighborhoods. Elementary students rode free buses to school. High-school students were given special passes to be used on the city's buses and subways.

Few school districts in any part of the country rushed to carry out the Supreme Court's 1954 decision. The Court was partly to blame for this. It didn't put a limit on how much time schools could take to desegregate [end segregation]. The greatest hostility to desegregating schools came from the South. Some southern states even passed laws that made it illegal to follow the Court's ruling. The state of Virginia planned what it called "massive resistance." Part of that resistance called for closing the public schools and opening private schools for whites only. Private schools weren't included in the Supreme Court's decision on "separate but equal."

In Little Rock, Arkansas, the issue of school desegregation exploded into a major crisis. The school board and the superintendent of schools in Little Rock agreed to go along with the 1954 ruling soon after it was announced. They developed a plan to open two all-white senior high schools to blacks by 1956. Junior-high and elementary schools would be integrated shortly afterward. But the school board changed its decision because its members began to hear from whites who opposed the plan. Some of those who were against the plan were disturbed by the possibility of black and white children dancing together at school events. In fact, any shared school activity was cause for concern. The thought of black children kissing white children in a school play, for example, horrified these people.

In response to these concerns, the school board developed a new plan. One school, Central High School, would be integrated in 1957. Little Rock's other schools would be desegregated over the following six years. Seventy-five black students wanted to attend Central High School. The school board, however, chose only nine: Minniejean Brown, Elizabeth Eckford, Ernest Green, Thelma Mothershed, Melba Patillo, Gloria Ray, Terrance Roberts, Jefferson Thomas, and Carlotta Walls. These students became known as the Little Rock Nine.

September 3, 1957 was to be the first day of school in Little Rock. On that day, the governor of Arkansas, Orval Faubus, placed 250 soldiers from the Arkansas National Guard around Central High. They had been told to keep everyone out, both whites and blacks. As far as Governor Faubus was concerned, white children were better off missing school than going to one that had black children in it.

School was then scheduled to begin the next day, September 4. The parents of the Little Rock Nine couldn't take their children to Central High because the school board felt that their presence might cause a riot. Arrangements had been made for police cars to drive the nine students to Central. Daisy Bates, an associate of Ella Baker and the head of the Arkansas branch of the NAACP, was going to accompany the students along with the police. Bates called the students to tell them where they should meet the police cars. She couldn't reach Elizabeth Eckford, however, because the Eckford family didn't have a phone.

On the morning of September 4, Elizabeth went to Central High alone. When she got off the bus near the school, she saw a crowd of white people and the Arkansas National Guard. In describing her experience that morning, Elizabeth later said:

> ...I walked across the street conscious of the crowd that stood there, but they moved away from me. [Then] the crowd began to follow me, calling me names. I still wasn't afraid, just a little bit nervous. Then my knees started to shake all of a sudden....Even so, I wasn't too scared because...I kept thinking that the [guards] would protect me...the guards let some white students go through [into the school]....I walked up to the guard who had let [them] in. He didn't move. When I tried to squeeze past him, he raised his bayonet and then the other guards moved in and raised their bayonets....Somebody started yelling, "Lynch her! Lynch her!"

Elizabeth ran toward a bus stop. The white mob followed. She heard them screaming, "No nigger...is going to get in our school!" Intent on a lynching, one of them shouted, "Drag her over to this tree!" Fortunately, a white woman pulled Elizabeth from the crowd and the two of them got away on a bus. For a long time, Elizabeth would have nightmares about her experience at Central High School on September 4, 1957.

When the eight other black students arrived with the police and Daisy Bates, the Arkansas National Guard also prevented them from entering Central. As the days went by, the guardsmen continued to follow Governor Faubus's orders to keep the Little Rock Nine out of school.

On September 14, President Dwight D. Eisenhower had a meeting with Governor Faubus. By the end of their discussion, the president thought he had convinced the governor to remove the National Guard from Central High, but they remained. The next time the Little Rock Nine tried to go to school, nearly

Arkansas National Guardsmen prevent four of the Little Rock Nine from entering Central High.

1,000 whites gathered outside in an angry mob. For their own protection, the children were driven home.

Finally, on September 24, President Eisenhower sent 1,000 U.S. soldiers into Little Rock. On the following day, the nine students entered Central High escorted by U.S. soldiers. The soldiers remained at Central for the entire school year. But Governor Faubus hadn't given up. During the next school year, he closed all of the high schools in Little Rock. The schools were opened again in 1959, and every one of them was integrated.

After the Supreme Court said in 1954 that racially separate schools were not legal, a number of blacks came to feel that the Court's decision may not have applied only to schools. Maybe the Court's ruling meant that other forms of segregation were also not legal.

In 1955, even before the crisis at Little Rock, segregation laws were tested in Alabama. That year, Ella Baker worked on New York City's school segregation problem, but she also played a role in what happened in Alabama.

IT STARTS IN MONTGOMERY

> *If you will protest courageously, and yet with dignity and Christian love, when the history books are written... the historians will have to say... 'There lived a great people—a black people—who injected new meaning and dignity into the veins of civilization.'*

DR. MARTIN LUTHER KING, JR.

During the time Ella Baker was traveling through the South for the NAACP, she met a woman by the name of Rosa Parks. Parks was a member and an officer of the NAACP's branch in Montgomery, Alabama. Whenever Baker was in town, the two women worked together, usually on the Leadership Conference. The conference was a program that had been started to help local members develop their ability to lead NAACP projects. Parks helped Baker to prepare written materials and also provided her with a list of the problems that concerned the Montgomery NAACP. These problems were discussed in the conference, along with the steps that might be taken to correct them.

On December 1, 1955, Rosa Parks left work and went shopping at a drugstore in Montgomery. Afterward she boarded a bus and took a seat. As more and more passengers got on, they all found seats except for one white man. The bus driver told Parks to stand so that the white man could sit. She refused and remained seated. The driver then called the police. Parks was arrested and taken to jail. There she was officially charged with violating Montgomery's bus segregation law.

In Alabama and other southern states, buses were segregated. In Montgomery, black passengers couldn't sit in the first 10 rows, which were reserved for whites only. They also couldn't sit in front of or next to a white person. Even if they were sitting in the section for black riders, blacks could be made to give up their seats if the white section was filled.

Parks may have been tired from work and shopping that day, but that's not why she wouldn't give up her seat. As she said later: "I was thinking that the only way to let them know I felt I was being mistreated was to do just what I did—resist the order [to stand]. . . . I simply decided that I would not get up. I had felt for a long time that if I was ever told to get up so a white person could sit, that I would refuse to do so."

Twelve years earlier, Parks had refused to obey another bus law. This law required blacks to pay their fares in the front of the bus, get off, and enter through the back door. This law was very insulting to blacks, and to make matters worse, white bus drivers sometimes drove away before blacks could get back on the bus. After paying her fare in the front of the bus, Parks refused to get off and enter at the back door. Because she refused, the bus driver threw her off the bus. Oddly enough, this bus driver was the same one who had Parks arrested in 1955.

Rosa Parks's many years of involvement with the NAACP's fight for equal rights certainly would have given her the courage to do these things. She had another source of inspiration, however. The summer before her arrest, Parks was a student at the Highlander Folk School in Tennessee. Highlander had been started in the 1930s to teach people—both blacks and whites—how to be social activists. In other words, Highlander taught individuals how to organize efforts that could change the way people thought and lived. For Parks and other blacks, change meant getting rid of segregation.

E. D. Nixon, a former president of the Montgomery NAACP, found out about Parks being jailed shortly after the incident took place. Her arrest gave him good reason to believe that the time had come to fight bus segregation. Nixon quickly arranged a meeting with Montgomery's black leaders, most of whom were ministers.

Jo Ann Robinson of the Women's Political Council, a black community-action group in Montgomery, also heard about Parks's arrest. Like Nixon, the council had been looking for a long time for way to challenge bus segregation. Council leaders decided to call for a bus boycott—a refusal to use the city's buses. Robinson quickly wrote and printed leaflets asking the black people of Montgomery not to ride the city's buses for one day. High-school and college students gave out the leaflets in black neighborhoods throughout the city.

By the time the ministers met, most of Montgomery's African Americans knew about the planned boycott. The ministers agreed to go along with the plan, and in their Sunday sermons they urged church members not to ride the buses.

The day of the boycott arrived. Of the thousands of blacks who normally used the city's buses, less than a dozen got on that day. Only a few whites rode the buses as well. The boycott was a success.

On the same day as the boycott, Parks's trial took place. The judge found her guilty of violating Montgomery's bus laws. After paying a $10 fine and court costs, Parks was released.

Immediately after the trial, the black ministers got together again and formed an organization to continue the boycott. They called it the Montgomery Improvement Association (MIA). The Reverend Martin Luther King, Jr., of the Dexter Avenue Baptist Church was chosen as the MIA's president. That night, when 5,000 blacks gathered in and around Montgomery's Holt Street Baptist Church for a meeting, they were asked if they wanted the boycott to go on. "Yes!" rang out 5,000 voices.

Black taxicab drivers agreed to carry boycotters for 10 cents, the same fare charged by buses. But the city ordered the drivers to charge the usual cab fare of 45 cents. The members of the MIA therefore formed their own car pool. More than 150 people volunteered their cars for use in the boycott.

By January, MIA officers had met with city and bus-company officials four times, but nothing had been settled. Since many more blacks than whites took buses, the boycott was indeed causing the bus company to lose a lot of money. In spite of this, the company and the city insisted on keeping the buses segregated.

In an attempt to end the boycott, however, city officials soon took action. Hoping to trick black riders back onto the buses, the mayor of Montgomery got a local newspaper to print a false report saying the boycott was over. But immediately after the report appeared, the MIA sent word to the black community that the boycott was still on. The city then tried to discourage the boycotters by harassing them. A number of blacks lost their jobs because they took part in the boycott. Police officers chased boycotters away from car-pool stations as they waited for rides. Car-pool drivers were constantly given driving violation tickets, often for charges that weren't true. Dr. King himself was arrested for speeding and taken to jail. He would have spent the night there, but the police released him when a crowd of protesters gathered outside.

Some whites reacted to the boycott in even more violent ways. MIA members received death threats over the phone. Boycotters were beaten on the streets. The homes of Dr. King and E. D. Nixon were bombed. Despite the attempt on his life,

King urged blacks in Montgomery to continue to protest peacefully.

In February 1956, the lawyers for the boycotters brought a case against Montgomery's segregated buses to a federal court. They were hoping that the 1954 Supreme Court ruling on schools might also be used to desegregate buses. During the same month, the city also went to court and claimed that the boycotters had broken a state of Alabama law that did not permit boycotts. Nearly 100 boycott leaders, including Dr. King, were ordered to appear in court.

Throughout all this, the blacks of Montgomery still refused to ride the buses. But money to run the boycott was getting low. There were lawyers' fees to be paid. In addition to the rising legal fees, the costs of gas, oil, and repairs for the car pool came to $3,000 a week. As a result of nationwide TV and newspaper stories about Montgomery, individuals and groups began to send money to help the boycotters. One of these groups was an organization called In Friendship.

In Friendship was formed in New York by Ella Baker and her friends A. Philip Randolph, Bayard Rustin, and Stanley Levison. Randolph and Rustin were leading black activists. Levison was a white attorney who had become very involved in the struggle of African Americans for equal rights. In Friendship held events to raise funds for the Montgomery boycotters and other southern blacks who were fighting for their rights. One such event took place at New York City's Madison Square Garden in 1956. Money from that event helped to pay the legal fees of the boycotters. In Friendship also gave money to buy new cars for the car pool.

The boycotters received good news from the federal court where the MIA had taken their case against Montgomery's bus segregation law. The court ruled that the city had to get rid of the law. This ruling made Montgomery's officials very angry. They had the right to take their case to the Supreme Court for another ruling, and that's what they did. This was exactly what the members of the MIA wanted. Surely the Supreme Court would rule in their favor. But it would be some time before the Court decided on the MIA's case. Until then, blacks continued the boycott.

Meanwhile, on November 13, 1956, the city got a state court to ban the car pool. This meant that the boycotters would have no transportation and might have to give up the boycott. On that very same day, however, the Supreme Court ruled that bus segregation in Montgomery, and in the entire state of Alabama, violated the Constitution of the United States. The bus segregation law, therefore, was unconstitutional. The boycotters had won! On December 20, 1956, the Supreme Court's decision became law and the boycott ended. The next day, the blacks of Montgomery went back to riding buses and sat wherever they wanted to sit.

The boycott lasted for 381 days. It provided future protesters with two valuable lessons: the force of mass action and the power of nonviolent resistance. Thousands of black Mont-

The Montgomery bus boycott ended in victory for African Americans throughout the state.

gomerians joining together to fight a common problem had created a powerful mass action. They had resisted an unfair law peacefully, even when they met with violence, and had shown that nonviolent resistance could change that law. They could have destroyed the buses or attacked those who opposed the boycott. Instead, they simply refused to ride until the law was changed.

The boycott proved that mass action and nonviolent resistance could work. It also demonstrated the ability of black churches and black church members to pull people together. Dr. King was a minister, as were many of the MIA's members. In fact, southern churches of all denominations had always been the center of black southern life. Churches were the main source of the South's African-American leaders.

In Friendship's support of the boycott gave Ella Baker the opportunity to speak often with Dr. King. After the boycott ended, she talked to him about starting a movement that would fight for the rights of African Americans throughout the South.

THE BLACK SOUTH GETS ITS OWN

  ...there is no middle ground for us. We must either have all the rights of American citizens, or we must be exterminated, for we can never again be slaves; nor can we cease to trouble the American people while any right enjoyed by others is denied or withheld from us.

FREDERICK DOUGLASS, abolitionist, writer, and former slave

When the Montgomery bus boycott ended, Ella Baker and other members of In Friendship hoped that a strong protest movement for the rights of African Americans would continue throughout the South. Since the U.S. Supreme Court's decision outlawed segregation only in Alabama, there were bus boycotts in Birmingham and Mobile, Alabama, and in Tallahassee, Florida. But Baker wasn't satisfied with this small amount of protest activity. She felt that a movement couldn't survive with just a few protests here and there. What was needed was one central organization that would provide direction for an all-out attack on every kind of racial discrimination in the South.

The leaders of the Montgomery boycott obviously knew how to organize and win. They had learned a lot from their struggle in Montgomery. Why, then, weren't they taking what they had learned and using it to organize blacks throughout the South? This is what Ella Baker asked Martin Luther King, Jr., "I irritated [him] with the question," she said. "His [response] was that after a big demonstration, there was [a] natural letdown and a need for people to sort of catch their breath. I didn't quite agree."

Ella Baker didn't agree because she believed in action. She thought people should never let up when there was a goal to fight for and reach. Baker and several members of In Friendship met with King. They pointed out that the success of the Montgomery boycott had made southern blacks ready to challenge every kind of segregation, not just bus segregation. King's reputation as the leader of the boycott gave him the power to unite other southern black leaders to fight Jim Crow laws. They convinced him. King called a meeting of the South's black leaders that would take place in Atlanta, Georgia, on January 11, 1957.

On January 10, the night before the meeting in Atlanta, a series of bombings took place in Montgomery. One destroyed the home of Rev. Robert S. Graetz, a white MIA member. A second bomb had been planted in his yard, but it failed to go off. Rev. Ralph Abernathy, who was at the Atlanta meeting, learned that his home had also been bombed that night. So had his church, as well as three other African-American churches.

Shaken by the violence, Dr. King and Rev. Ralph Abernathy left before the meeting to investigate the bombings. Ella Baker and Bayard Rustin stayed in Atlanta to manage the conference with Dr. King's wife, Coretta, and Rev. Fred Shuttlesworth. More than 60 ministers showed up. This was the beginning of a new civil rights organization—the Southern Christian Leadership Conference (SCLC). Dr. King became the SCLC's president. Rev. Ralph Abernathy was named its treasurer.

Never before had there been such an organization in the South. A number of southern towns had local groups or organizations that worked to end discrimination. But this was the first time that just one organization had tried to unite all of these efforts throughout the South. It was common to hear whites in the South say that blacks there were happy with the Jim Crow way of life. Blacks resisted that way of life, whites claimed, only when they were pushed to do so by "outside agitators" such as the NAACP. The formation of the SCLC gave notice to southern whites that southern blacks knew Jim Crow segregation was wrong. Now the blacks themselves, without being "agitated" by others, were beginning to fight for a better life.

The SCLC was an organization of organizations. An individual could not join the SCLC. Its members were other organizations—churches and groups that had formed to fight racial prejudice. Some of the SCLC's member organizations included the Inter Civil Council of Tallahassee, Florida, led by Rev. C. K. Steele; the Mobile (Alabama) Interdenominational Ministerial Alliance, whose president was Rev. Joseph Lowery; and the Alabama Christian Movement for Human Rights in Birmingham, headed by Rev. Fred Shuttlesworth. In addition to leading their own organizations, Steele, Lowery, and Shuttlesworth became officers of the SCLC.

By late summer of 1957, the SCLC had begun to talk about launching a Crusade for Citizenship. The crusade's purpose would be to increase the number of blacks who were registered to vote. At that time, less than 10 percent of southern blacks voted—not because they didn't want to vote, but because it was dangerous for them to do so. Just a couple of years earlier, Rev. George Lee had been shot to death in Mississippi after trying to register black voters. If they weren't killed, blacks who tried to vote were often beaten or fired from their jobs.

Southern whites knew that the power to change Jim Crow laws rested in the hands of the people who voted. In order to get elected, politicians would have to please most of the voters. Until now, white voters had always outnumbered black voters, so whites had more political power. In other words, whites had the power to make laws that benefited them and kept blacks "in their place." If black people began voting in great numbers, politicians would also have to please them in order to win an election.

The easiest way to please black voters, of course, was to change the Jim Crow laws. But this was a change that many whites didn't want. They knew that as long as blacks didn't vote, politicians wouldn't listen to them—and Jim Crow laws would remain. As a result, they came up with ways of keeping African Americans from voting. One of these ways was to prevent blacks from registering. Many blacks in the South had to take a literacy test before they could register to vote. They had to read and explain very difficult parts of the U.S. Constitution or other legal documents. Such material was rarely given to whites to read. Since a large number of blacks in southern farm areas were unable to read or write, whites knew that they wouldn't be able to pass the test. This would stop them from registering.

During that summer, the Civil Rights Act of 1957 was passed. It was the first civil rights act to be passed since 1875. One of the purposes of the act was to help African Americans register to vote. It gave the federal government the right to sue southern registration offices if they kept any blacks from voting because of race. The government could sue for an individual and would also pay the court costs. Before this act, if someone wanted to sue because of racial discrimination, he or she had to pay the legal expenses. These fees usually prevented poor blacks from achieving their right to vote through the courts.

The Civil Rights Act of 1957 also established the Civil Rights Commission. The commission was formed to study racial conditions in the United States and inform the president of its findings. However, many African Americans weren't satisfied. They didn't feel that this act gave the government enough power to enforce the rights of African Americans. It wasn't clear how much this new act would help blacks in their efforts to change laws involving segregation and voting rights. But the Act showed that the federal government was aware of the need to help blacks in their fight against racial discrimination. It encouraged the SCLC's leaders to move ahead with the organization's voter registration program, the Crusade for Citizenship.

The SCLC knew that blacks would have to start voting together in order to fight unjust laws. For this reason, the organization planned to get its crusade off the ground. It planned to hold 22 rallies in 22 southern cities on the same day, February 12, 1958. Someone was needed to coordinate the rallies, or put everything together. But as late as January, the SCLC still had no one who could do the job. There was very little time before the rallies were scheduled to take place. Finally, Dr. King asked Ella Baker to return to Atlanta and take charge of preparations for the SCLC.

Her travels in the South for the NAACP made her well suited for the job that had to be done. During those travels, she had gotten to know many of the minister-leaders in the 22 cities of the crusade. She now contacted those leaders to let them know about the rallies. She suggested that they give their church members information on the rallies as part of the Sunday sermons. She also prepared programs for the events that would take place at each rally. She wrote and sent out information packages. She researched the voter registration laws in each of the southern states where rallies were to be held, and she passed that information on to rally organizers. She also offered advice on overcoming those registration laws. Ella Baker did all of this within only four weeks.

"The word *crusade* [means] for me a vigorous movement," Baker said, "with high purpose and involving masses of people." The rallies, however, did not result in getting large numbers of

Workers practice registering voters during the SCLC's Crusade for Citizenship.

blacks registered. Some blamed the NAACP for this. Several of the ministers who led member organizations in the SCLC also belonged to the NAACP. It was said that the NAACP leaders advised those ministers not to cooperate with the SCLC's Crusade for Citizenship. The NAACP was afraid of losing its position as the major civil rights organization if the SCLC was successful. That loss of position would mean a loss of money. The SCLC's success would attract contributions of money from people who might have contributed to the NAACP. Both organizations needed large amounts of funds in order to continue their protest efforts.

Ella Baker, however, felt that the SCLC itself was to be blamed for the failure of the crusade. She believed that the SCLC had mobilized people—gotten them moving—but hadn't organized them. Voter clinics, where people could learn how to register and use voting machines, were supposed to be a part of the crusade program. But very few clinics had been set up.

Little attention had been given to making sure people were taken to and from registration offices. It was like asking people who knew nothing about basketball to sign up for a basketball team but not giving them a ball or showing them how to play the game.

Four days after the rallies, Ella Baker went back to New York. Her temporary assignment was over. A month later, she returned to Atlanta to work for the SCLC again. During the year since the SCLC had been founded, nothing much had been done to organize its office. This was mainly because the SCLC didn't have an executive director. Baker now took on the responsibility of getting the office set up and running smoothly.

There was much to be done, and few people to do it. As a result, Baker did just about everything—from the work of an executive to the work of a clerk. She made decisions on how the office should be set up. She did the mimeographing (a way to make copies). She typed her own letters, filed, and answered phones. She did anything that would get the office functioning as an office should. But her tremendous ability to organize for social change—to help change the conditions of people's lives— was going unused.

Ella Baker soon found herself in a difficult situation. After several weeks of working at the SCLC, there was still no executive director. Without an executive director, many important decisions and plans of action could not be made. Eager to get things rolling, Baker suggested to the SCLC that a friend of hers, Rev. John Tilley, be considered for the position of executive director. Rev. John Tilley had just led a very successful voter-registration campaign in Baltimore, Maryland. Ella Baker arranged for Dr. King and other SCLC officers to meet with Rev. John Tilley. At the end of April 1958, the SCLC officially announced that Tilley was its executive director. Ella Baker became the associate director.

Tilley and Baker immediately began working on the SCLC's Crusade for Citizenship. In the southern towns and cities where the SCLC had member organizations, they set up workshops to give information on the crusade and advice on running voter-registration programs. Once again, however, the crusade did not produce as many black voters as expected. In addition to the competition between the NAACP and the SCLC, there was still strong white resistance to registration of blacks. Much of this resistance came from white people who worked at the registration offices. If there was no literacy test, other things were done to delay or prevent blacks from registering. Even when the crusade got a sizable number of blacks out to register, only a few succeeded in getting signed up. Ella Baker reported on what happened in Shreveport, Louisiana: "...250 persons crowded the Caddo Parish Courthouse in an attempt to register. Only 46 people were interviewed that day, and only 15 [were] registered."

Baker continued to feel that the crusade would have greater success if the SCLC developed a program that would actually organize its members and get them to work together closely. She believed that Dr. Martin Luther King, Jr., its president, was responsible for the fact that such a program hadn't been developed. King received countless requests to speak before various groups. He felt obligated to fulfill all of these requests. It was the best way to raise the money that the SCLC needed so badly. But his long absences from the office left the SCLC without the strong direction it needed. These difficulties strengthened one of Ella Baker's basic beliefs—that an organization should not have just one leader. An organization with only one leader becomes helpless when that leader isn't around or has no real ability to lead. Baker preferred organizations in which every member could be a leader and could contribute equally to reach the goals of the organization.

In April 1959, the ax fell. The SCLC's executive director, Rev. John Tilley, was blamed for the poor results of the Crusade for Citizenship and was fired. Ella Baker was named interim director. *Interim* meant that she would have the job until the SCLC found someone else to be the permanent executive director. "They asked me to serve as the director," she told an interviewer, "with a cut in whatever little salary I was getting, which is not new to me. You see...it was more important to go ahead. I may as well play the supporting role there as anywhere else. So I stayed on." Ella Baker's salary had been cut because the SCLC was facing a money problem.

This was the second time that the SCLC could have made Baker its executive director and didn't. It chose not to because she wasn't a minister. But, just as important, she was a woman. At that time, most men thought women didn't have the ability to be the heads of organizations or businesses—that they were better suited to be wives and mothers. As a woman, Baker knew that SCLC leaders looked upon her as someone who should take orders, not give them. She always said that she never tried to be a leader in the SCLC: "I . . . knew from the beginning that having a woman be an executive of SCLC was not something that would go over with the male-dominated leadership. And then, of course, my personality wasn't right. . . . I was not afraid to disagree with the higher authorities."

After her appointment as interim director, Ella Baker continued to work on the Crusade for Citizenship in South Carolina and Alabama. But response to the crusade was still discouraging. By September 1959, Baker had decided that it was time to put her thoughts about the SCLC's weaknesses on paper. She had already made many other suggestions for improving the organization's performance, and most of them had not been acted on. One of her ideas was to ask the Highlander Folk School to help in setting up Citizenship Schools for blacks who couldn't read or write. The Citizenship Schools would teach these people how to read and write as well as how to register and vote. (The SCLC didn't put this idea into action until after Ella Baker had left the organization.)

Baker wasn't sure how the SCLC would respond to any more suggestions from her, but she went ahead with her report. In it, she asked two questions: "Have we been so busy doing the things that had to be done, that we failed to [do] what should be done? Have we really come to grips with what it takes to do the job for which SCLC was organized; and are we willing to pay the price?"

Baker went on to list what she thought the SCLC had to do if it was to become a stronger and more effective organization.

She offered three main suggestions. First, the SCLC should create a plan that would unify the activities of all its member groups. Second, the people in the member groups who had demonstrated leadership ability should be given some help in developing that ability. Finally, the SCLC should have a program that organized black southerners to fight every form of discrimination—and this program should use mass action and nonviolent resistance to achieve its goals.

Ella Baker had always supported nonviolent resistance as a valuable weapon in the fight for civil rights. But she wasn't sure that she herself could resist in a nonviolent way. "Whether this is right or wrong or good or bad, I have already been conditioned," she said, "and I have not seen anything in the nonviolent technique that can [persuade me against] challenging someone who wants to step on my neck. If necessary, if they hit me, I might hit them back."

King agreed with Ella Baker's list of suggestions. The SCLC's board of directors set up a committee to work on the list, and Baker was asked to meet with the committee to develop plans and programs for 1960. But 1960 would involve her in a way that had nothing to do with those plans and programs.

12 "BIGGER THAN A HAMBURGER"

❝I had no difficulty relating to the young people. I spoke their language in terms of the meaning of what they had to say. I didn't change my speech pattern and they didn't have to change their speech pattern. But we were able to communicate.❞

ELLA BAKER, in *Black Women in White America*

In 1960, four black college students did something that gave the civil rights movement new strength and brought another change in Ella Baker's life. The four young men—Ezell Blair, Jr., Franklin McCain, Joseph McNeil, and David Richmond—attended North Carolina Agricultural and Technical College (A & T) in Greensboro, North Carolina. For several days, the students thought about where and how they could organize a strike against segregation in their college town.

They decided to sit at the lunch counter at the local Woolworth's and ask for service. By doing something as simple as this, the students would challenge North Carolina's Jim Crow laws. Throughout the South at stores like Woolworth's, blacks could walk up and down the aisles and buy anything they wanted, but they couldn't sit in the dining area and get something to eat.

On February 1, 1960, the four students entered Woolworth's in Greensboro and took seats at the lunch counter. When they asked for coffee, the waitress told them, "We don't serve colored." This was the response they had expected. They remained seated until the store closed for the day.

What the four students did became known as a sit-in (sitting down and staying in a place marked for whites only as a protest against discrimination).

This was not the first sit-in. The Congress for Racial Equality (CORE) had organized sit-ins as early as 1942. Then in August 1958, another sit-in was staged at a large drugstore in Oklahoma City, Oklahoma. There Clara Luper, a black schoolteacher, and eight of her students, aged 5 through 15, sat at the lunch counter one Saturday until the police took them away. Luper did this every Saturday with different students for several years. However, the national news media didn't report on those earlier sit-ins as they would the ones in Greensboro.

News of the Greensboro sit-in quickly reached the A & T campus. The next day the four students at Woolworth's were joined by other students. As the week went on, students from high schools and other colleges in the area also participated.

Young college students in other parts of the South soon learned about the Greensboro sit-ins by word of mouth and from newspaper and TV reports. They began their own sit-in demonstrations. Most of those sitting-in were black, but some were white students. All of them stuck to the principle of nonviolent resistance, although they received horrible treatment. Angry whites dumped ketchup, sugar, and hot coffee on their heads. They crushed burning cigarettes into their necks. Young women were dragged by their hair off the stools. Many of the demonstrators were arrested or jailed. But despite all of this, by the end of March, thousands of students had taken part in sit-ins in more than a dozen southern towns and cities.

Ella Baker immediately realized the importance of the sit-ins. The civil rights movement hadn't shown such energy and determination since the Montgomery bus boycott. She was excited about the support young people could give to the movement. Baker realized, however, that the young people needed a sense of unity and a program that would include lunch-counter protests as well as protests against other forms of discrimination.

Baker felt the students should have the opportunity to get together and to develop their own plan of action. She therefore asked the SCLC for $800 to sponsor a meeting of students who had been involved in the sit-ins. She recalled: "It hadn't gone on so long before I suggested that we call a conference of the sit-inners. . . . It was very obvious to the Southern Christian Leadership Conference that there was little or no communication between those who sat in, say, in Charlotte, North Carolina, and those who sat in at some other place in Virginia or Alabama. They were motivated [inspired] by what the North Carolina four had started, but they were not in contact with each other . . . you couldn't build a sustaining [lasting] force just based on spontaneity [spur-of-the-moment thinking]."

Ella Baker arranged with the school from which she had graduated—Shaw University in Raleigh, North Carolina—to host the meeting over the Easter weekend in April 1960. She expected 100 students.

Close to 300 students—both black and white—showed up. In addition, there were representatives from the three leading civil rights groups—the NAACP, the SCLC, and CORE. Begun in 1942, CORE was more interracial than either the NAACP or the SCLC. For years, CORE had concentrated its efforts on ending racial discrimination in the North. But since the start of the civil rights movement, its activities had turned more and more to the South.

The students at the three-day meeting at Shaw would have to choose between remaining separate or becoming part of one of the three organizations represented at the meeting. The NAACP hoped to persuade the students to join with it. CORE also wanted the students, and so did the SCLC. Baker believed the young people should make their own decisions and be free to form their own independent group if they chose to do so.

While the students met to talk about what they would do, King called a meeting of SCLC people, including Baker. The purpose of the discussion was to decide how the SCLC could take over the student movement.

Since Ella Baker was in favor of the students' remaining independent, the discussion turned into a heated argument that had a dramatic ending. In describing what happened, Baker said: "The Southern Christian Leadership Conference felt that they could influence how things went [with the students]. They were interested in having the students become an arm of SCLC.

They were most confident that this would be their baby, because I [was the one who] called the meeting.... Well, I disagreed. I wasn't one to say yes, because it came from the Reverend King. So when it was proposed, that [SCLC] could influence... what [the students] wanted done, I was outraged. I walked out."

The students did decide to create their own organization—the Student Nonviolent Coordinating Committee (SNCC, pronounced *snick*). Ella Baker later said that the students had made up their minds that they would remain independent even before the meeting at Shaw took place. But they might have weakened under the pressure of the three big organizations if Baker hadn't encouraged them to form their own group. In an article for a publication called *The Southern Patriot*, Baker wrote: "The [Raleigh meeting] made it crystal clear that... sit-ins and other demonstrations are concerned with something bigger than a hamburger or a giant-sized coke.... the Negro and white students, North and South, are seeking to rid America of the scourge of racial segregation and discrimination—not only at lunch counters, but in every aspect of life."

The students didn't forget Ella Baker's strong encouragement. She became their adviser and set up the main SNCC office in Atlanta. Within two years, she had helped to organize two major civil rights groups—the SCLC and SNCC. In August 1960, Baker resigned from the SCLC in order to devote most of her energies to SNCC. Since SNCC couldn't pay her, Baker earned an income by working for Atlanta's Young Women's Christian Association (YWCA). She was the director of a project that had been started to create better racial understanding between black and white college students in the South. To accomplish this, Baker set up workshops that brought black and white students together at various southern schools. These workshops discussed the civil rights movement and how the events of the movement related to the students. SNCC members often took part in the talks.

Ella Baker's influence on SNCC could be seen in the way its

members handled the idea of leadership. Officers were elected, but they weren't the leaders. The leadership was made up of the entire SNCC group. In fact, their slogan was "We are all leaders." This was in keeping with Baker's thinking about who should lead any organization—not one person but everyone in that organization.

Ella Baker described her role as adviser to SNCC as one that involved asking questions. She also urged SNCC members to raise questions so that they would have a clear picture of any action they planned to take. "I usually tried to present whatever participation I had in terms of questions, and tried to get people to reach certain decisions by questioning some of the things themselves," she said.

Baker attended all SNCC meetings when important issues were being discussed. These meetings often lasted not hours but days. According to Baker, comfort wasn't a major concern: "The structure of SNCC finally got hammered out by having long meetings.... The first time I ever remember having a charley horse in my leg was after 30 hours that I had been more or less sitting in the . . . same position."

Miss Ella, as the SNCC people called Baker, became famous for playing her "little trick" at meetings. Because she believed that everyone had something to contribute in making decisions, Baker was always on the alert for someone who wasn't speaking up. She would then settle herself next to that person and ask what he or she thought about what was going on. The person would tell her. Then she would raise his or her hand and shout, "Look, here's somebody with something to say about that."

Ella Baker was a protective angel, according to Bob Moses, who became a SNCC legend because of his gentleness and great courage. Remembering Baker, Moses said: "It was Ella more than anyone else who gave us the space to operate in. As long as she was sitting there in the meetings, no one else could dare come in and say I think you should do this or that, because no one could pull rank on her. Her stature was such that there

Bob Moses, field secretary of the Student Nonviolent Coordinating Committee.

wasn't anyone from the NAACP to Dr. King who could get by her. I think that the actual course of the SNCC movement is a testimony to the fact that the students were left free to develop on their own. That was her real contribution."

Baker tried never to interfere at SNCC meetings, and if she did, it was only when she felt that it was absolutely necessary. One such occasion came during a meeting held at the Highlander School. SNCC was trying to decide on what kind of protest activity it should get into—direct action or voter registration. Direct action (such as a peaceful sit-in or boycott) appealed to some members because of the danger it presented. Danger meant white hostility. The goal of direct action was, in fact, to stir up such extreme white hostility that the federal government would be forced to pass new laws guaranteeing the civil rights of blacks.

SNCC members who favored voter registration pointed out what the vote meant to black people. It meant power that would enable blacks to choose government officials who would help the black cause. Neither side would give in to the other. The talk became so heated that SNCC seemed to be splitting into two different groups. "They broke up into a kind of fight—a pulling apart," recalled Baker: "I never intervened between the struggle if I could avoid it. Most of the youngsters had been trained...to follow adults....I felt they ought to have a chance to learn to think things through and to make the decisions. But this was a point at which I did have something to say."

Baker ended the conflict by suggesting something rather simple. Why not do both? she asked. Some SNCC volunteers could go into direct action, while others worked for voter registration. They agreed. Eventually they would all learn that voter registration was just as dangerous and received just as much attention as did direct action.

On the direct-action side, a number of SNCC workers became involved in Freedom Rides. This project was begun by CORE. Freedom Rides were intended to pressure the federal government into making southern states obey a 1960 Supreme Court ruling. In that ruling, the Supreme Court said that interstate buses and trains (those carrying passengers from one state to another) could not be segregated. The Court had also ruled that lunch counters and restrooms in the terminals used by interstate buses and trains could not be segregated. The South, however, had ignored the ruling. On Freedom Rides, teams of blacks and whites traveled together through the South on buses. They challenged segregated seating on the buses and segregation in bus terminal facilities.

Freedom Riders sit in a whites-only waiting room in the Montgomery bus terminal.

The first Freedom Ride began on May 4, 1961. Six whites and seven blacks left Washington, D.C., for New Orleans, Louisiana. When their bus stopped at the terminal in Rock Hill, South Carolina, a mob of white men beat two of the black Freedom Riders for trying to use the whites-only restroom.

In Atlanta, the 13 Freedom Riders divided into two groups. One group left Atlanta on a Greyhound bus; the other group left on a Trailways bus. At the terminal in Anniston, Alabama, a crowd of white men smashed the windows of the Greyhound bus and slashed its tires. With its passengers still aboard, the bus pulled out of the terminal to avoid more damage. When a flat tire forced the bus to stop, white attackers threw a firebomb into it. The driver and all of the passengers escaped through an emergency exit just before the bus burst into flames.

The Freedom Riders suffered a few cuts and bruises and were taken to a hospital. Hundreds of whites surrounded the hospital and prevented the Riders from leaving. White police officers were there, but they wouldn't help. Finally, the Riders were rescued by a group of blacks from Birmingham. They were led by Rev. Fred Shuttlesworth of the SCLC.

Freedom Riders on the Trailways bus also faced trouble in Anniston, but things were worse for them in Birmingham. There, a mob of white men beat them with metal pipes and baseball bats. The police finally appeared after the worst of the violence had taken place. It was believed that Birmingham's commissioner of public safety, Eugene "Bull" Connor, had made a deal with the mob. Some people have said that he allowed the whites to have 20 minutes with the Riders before sending in his police officers.

Both groups of Freedom Riders reached Birmingham. But they couldn't go on to New Orleans because the bus drivers refused to take them. The Riders therefore continued to New Orleans by plane. It looked as though the Freedom Rides would die. Diane Nash, who was in charge of SNCC's direct-action activities, said that she couldn't let that happen. In describing her feelings, Nash said: "If the Freedom Rides had been stopped as the result of violence, I strongly felt that the future of the movement was going to be cut short. The impression would have been that whenever a movement starts, all [you have to do] is attack it with massive violence and the blacks [will] stop."

SNCC sent 10 new Riders—8 blacks and 2 whites—to Birmingham for the remaining part of the journey to New Orleans. But the bus drivers still refused to carry them. "Bull" Connor had the 10 Freedom Riders arrested. He claimed that he did it "for their own safety."

The federal government now became involved. U.S. officials talked the governor of Alabama, John Patterson, into allowing the Riders to leave Birmingham by bus. Patterson agreed to supply the Freedom Riders with police protection while the bus was on the road to Montgomery and at the terminal in Montgomery, where the bus was scheduled to make a stop. At the Montgomery city limits, the police escort disapeared. The bus pulled into the terminal, and the Freedom Riders were attacked by a crowd of white men. Angry that Patterson hadn't kept his word, President John F. Kennedy sent federal marshals

THE ROUTE OF THE FREEDOM RIDERS 1961

ATLANTIC OCEAN

GULF OF MEXICO

MAY 4, Departure

Washington, D.C.
Richmond
Petersburg
VIRGINIA
WEST VIRGINIA
Lynchburg
Danville
NORTH CAROLINA
Durham
May 8
May 7
Charlotte
Rock Hill
Winnsboro
May 10
SOUTH CAROLINA
Augusta
May 9
Atlanta
GEORGIA
Anniston
KENTUCKY
TENNESSEE
May 14
May 14
Birmingham
ALABAMA
Montgomery
May 20
FLORIDA
Meridian
MISSISSIPPI
Jackson
May 24
LOUISIANA
ARKANSAS
New Orleans

N
W E
S

0   100   200
miles

to Montgomery to protect the Freedom Riders and to keep order.

Seventeen more Freedom Riders joined the 10 in Montgomery. The 27 Riders left that city on May 24 in two buses headed for New Orleans. The buses crossed the Alabama state line and entered Mississippi. At the Jackson bus terminal, the Freedom Riders were arrested for using the whites-only facilities. At their trial in court, they were found guilty of violating the state's segregation laws and sent to prison for 60 days.

The Freedom Rides would not be stopped, however. More and more Freedom Riders kept going south, and they continued to be arrested and jailed in Mississippi. The Freedom Rides finally ended in September 1961, when the Interstate Commerce Commission (ICC) issued an order. The ICC is an agency of the federal government. Its order gave more strength to the 1960 Supreme Court ruling. The ICC ruling ended segregation on all interstate buses and trains as well as in lunch rooms, waiting rooms, and rest rooms in interstate terminals. The South now had a law it could not ignore.

The young people of SNCC received much of the credit for the victory that had been won by the Freedom Riders. Like everyone involved in the civil rights movement, they were courageous and dedicated to achieving equal rights.

Ella Baker had been right in believing that the energy and determination of the young would make the movement more powerful. As SNCC went on to new battles, Baker continued to give valuable support and advice.

13 MISSISSIPPI, A MARCH, AND MORE

66 *Segregation now!*
Segregation tomorrow!
Segregation forever. **99**

GEORGE WALLACE, Governor
of Alabama, 1963

While some SNCC volunteers were going on Freedom Rides, other members of SNCC were working on voter registration. Along with the SCLC's Crusade for Citizenship, their efforts greatly increased what was being done to obtain voting rights for blacks.

To help its workers, SNCC provided them with detailed maps of the areas they would be covering. The maps showed where the sheriff's office, post office, and other public buildings in each work area were located. Like military troops about to enter enemy territory, the workers were drilled constantly.

SNCC made sure they knew the location of all roads, creeks and rivers, hills and valleys, and nearby towns. For in a way, these volunteers *were* soldiers—and, like soldiers, they had to know the landscape in case they actually had to run for their lives.

Ella Baker knew many black southerners through her work with the NAACP and the SCLC. She was therefore able to provide SNCC registration volunteers with the names of people to contact in the areas where they would be working. These contacts were very important because they made it easier to meet people and get their support for SNCC projects.

Hundreds of black families allowed SNCC volunteers to live with them. In doing this, they risked jail or having their homes burned down. Often, to protect a SNCC worker asleep in the house, a member of the family sat up all night at a window, shotgun in hand.

For the most part, SNCC concentrated its voter-registration efforts in the smaller towns of the rural South, where most of the South's poor blacks lived. The blacks in these towns made a living from working on farms or in low-paying factory jobs. SNCC tried to identify with the poverty of the people. SNCC workers wore blue overalls or jeans. Their salary was only $10 per week.

Most of SNCC's voter registration projects took place in Georgia and Mississippi. In Mississippi, blacks made up almost half of the state's population, but only about 5 percent could vote.

In August 1961, Bob Moses began the first SNCC registration project in McComb, Mississippi. Two other SNCC members—Reginald Robinson and John Hardy—joined Moses. Together, they set up a school to teach McComb's blacks how to register. Volunteers went door-to-door to get people to attend the school and, afterward, to try to register. A dozen brave blacks did go to the school and then tried to register. Moses went to the registration office with them. There, they had to wait a long time before the voter-registration official paid any attention to them. The long wait was meant to discourage the 12 from registering. In the end, only two of them succeeded in getting registered to vote.

Black high-school students in McComb also took part in voter-registration activities. But they were more interested in desegregating the lunch counters at Woolworth's and the Greyhound bus terminal. SNCC set up a school to train these students in nonviolent protest. In August, two students—Curtis Hayes and Hollis Watkins—were jailed for 30 days after a sit-in at Woolworth's. Later that month, 15-year-old Brenda Travis participated in a sit-in at the lunch counter of the Greyhound bus terminal. This happened shortly before the ICC ordered interstate bus terminals to desegregate. Travis was arrested and put on trial. The judge sent her to a state school for delinquents. Older students who had sat in with her received eight-month jail terms.

In September, the students had their biggest demonstration. It came out of their anger at the death of Herbert Lee. Lee was an African-American farmer and the father of nine children. He had been driving Bob Moses around the area during the registration effort. Lee was found with a bullet in his head. The police picked up a white man for Lee's murder, but they let him go. One hundred black McComb high-school students marched to City Hall in protest. They were joined by Moses and other SNCC volunteers. At City Hall, marchers got down on their knees and prayed, and everyone was arrested.

When the students were released, their high-school principal warned them to stop demonstrating. In response, they turned in their books and stayed out of school. Moses and Charles McDew, who was then SNCC's executive chairman, set up Nonviolent High School to continue the education of the students. Here the students were taught the usual high-school subjects. However, they were also taught the differences in the way blacks and whites in the South lived and how the two races related to each other. There were studies on blacks in the North and discussions on whether northern blacks were completely free.

McComb's Nonviolent High lasted only a few weeks, but it became the model for the Freedom Schools that SNCC later developed in the South. For their work with young blacks in McComb, Moses and McDew were accused by town officials of contributing to the delinquency of minors—that is, encouraging children to break the law. They were arrested and sent to jail for four months.

In other parts of the South, other SNCC activists and their supporters were facing the same dangers that SNCC and local people experienced in McComb. Many were beaten or jailed, and some were killed.

Moses and McDew got out of jail and left Mississippi in December 1961. "We had, to put it mildly, got our feet wet," said Moses. "We now knew something of what it took to run a voter registration campaign in Mississippi. We knew some of the obstacles we would have to face; we had some general idea of what had to be done to get such a campaign started....And we began to set about doing this." Shortly after leaving McComb, Bob Moses became the director of voter registration for the Council of Federated Organizations (COFO). COFO was formed by SNCC, CORE, the NAACP, and the SCLC to coordinate voter-registration efforts in Mississippi.

In April 1963, Martin Luther King, Jr., and the SCLC began protest demonstrations in Birmingham, Alabama. The targets of the demonstrations were the city's large department stores. The SCLC wanted to desegregate lunch counters, elevators, and water fountains in these stores. It also wanted jobs for blacks as clerks and salespeople. The people of Birmingham were asked to boycott certain stores and take part in protest marches. About 80 percent of the city's blacks refused to shop in the stores that were marked for the boycott.

It was in Birmingham that the largest number of young people participated in civil rights demonstrations. Their ages

Young protesters in Birmingham are hosed under orders of Commissioner Bull Connor.

ranged from 6 to 18. Birmingham was an SCLC project, but the young people who took part in the marches received training in nonviolent resistance from SNCC workers. There was always the possibility that the young ones might be arrested and jailed. Still, the SCLC's James Bevel believed that young people were less afraid of going to jail than were adults because they didn't have jobs they might lose as a result of taking part in protests. Bevel also felt that news stories that showed youngsters being arrested would give Americans a good look at just how brutal things were for blacks in the South.

In early May, the first group of youths marched toward City Hall and were arrested. Minutes later, more students marched. When they, too, were arrested, a third group headed toward City Hall. The marches continued until almost 1,000 young people had been jailed by Birmingham's public safety commissioner, Eugene "Bull" Connor, and his police force.

The next day, hundreds more marched. This time, Connor met them with high-pressure water hoses (the kind used by fire fighters) and police dogs. The water knocked the marchers to the ground and threw them against cars and buildings. The dogs growled and lunged at the marchers' legs. More young marchers were carted off to jail.

Outraged by the use of fire hoses and dogs, adults joined the young people. The marches went on for a total of six days, and more than 2,500 people were arrested. Many of them had to be placed in outdoor pens because the jails were full. Eventually, the SCLC raised enough money to get all of them released.

Newspaper and TV reports on these events in Birmingham angered people across the United States. Many people got in touch with the federal government and urged that it help end the crisis in Birmingham. Members of the U.S. Department of Justice had been in Birmingham when the demonstrations began. They had been sent to help Dr. King come to an agreement with city officials.

Ella Baker also went to Birmingham. She was concerned about the young people and visited those who were in jail. She convinced them that their efforts were helping the cause and praised them for their courage. She was at the meeting when King offered to call a one-day truce, or break, in the marches after the sixth day. King believed that the brief truce would allow blacks and whites to reach a peaceful agreement. Since Baker had no official position, she couldn't say anything. She had gone to the meeting with the wife of Rev. Fred Shuttlesworth. Mrs. Shuttlesworth was taking her husband's place because he had been badly injured during one of the marches.

The SCLC had been meeting with Birmingham's white leaders during the entire time the marches were going on. Because of the boycott, store owners were losing money. TV coverage of police brutality deeply embarrassed them as well. They were therefore eager to come to an agreement. They soon agreed to desegregate. In addition, a committee would be set up to talk about future desegregation goals, such as the schools. This committee was very important because it provided oppor-

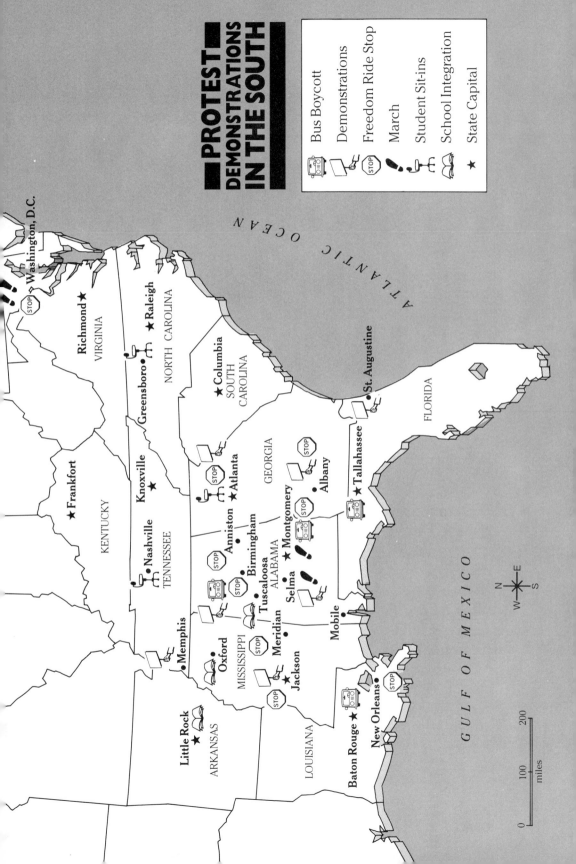

PROTEST DEMONSTRATIONS IN THE SOUTH

Bus Boycott
Demonstrations
Freedom Ride Stop
March
Student Sit-ins
School Integration
★ State Capital

ATLANTIC OCEAN

GULF OF MEXICO

Washington, D.C.

Richmond ★
VIRGINIA

★ Raleigh
Greensboro ●
NORTH CAROLINA

★ Columbia
SOUTH CAROLINA

St. Augustine

FLORIDA

★ Frankfort
KENTUCKY

Knoxville ★
Nashville ●
TENNESSEE

Atlanta
★ Atlanta
GEORGIA

Albany ●

★ Tallahassee

Anniston ●
Birmingham ●
Tuscaloosa ●
Selma ● Montgomery
ALABAMA

Memphis ●

Oxford ●
Meridian ●
MISSISSIPPI
Jackson ●

Mobile ●

★ Little Rock
ARKANSAS

LOUISIANA

★ Baton Rouge
New Orleans ●

N
W — E
S

0   100   200
miles

tunities for both blacks and whites to get together and openly discuss racial issues.

Ella Baker had stopped in Birmingham on her way to Louisville, Kentucky, where she would meet with her new employer, the Southern Conference Educational Fund (SCEF). Baker had completed her project with the Atlanta YWCA, and she was now a consultant for SCEF. Founded in Louisville in 1942, SCEF worked to improve relations between southern whites and blacks.

Ella Baker explained what she did as a consultant: "I'm something of a sounding board...a bridge...which means that when crises [emergencies] or situations arise...in black-white relationships, they are able to call upon whatever resources I have, in terms of having been around for a long while and knowing people. Also, it means attending board meetings and helping, hopefully, the adult members of the board to understand what some of the board members might think are the...too radical [extreme] approaches of the young people who are now doing the work of SCEF." People who knew Baker were familiar with her way of doing things. She wasn't there to take over and run things. She was there to help.

In June in Mississippi, white hatred again boiled over. Medgar Evers, an NAACP officer, was shot to death in the driveway of his home in Jackson. For many years, Evers had been active in civil rights efforts in Mississippi and other areas of the South. People across the nation were shocked and horrified by his murder. On the day of his funeral, hundreds of angry young blacks almost started a riot in Jackson. Later, his accused killer was arrested, put on trial, and set free. Because he had given his life for the black cause, Medgar Evers became a hero of the civil rights movement.

During the same summer, one of the greatest expressions of racial unity in the history of the United States took place. It was called the March on Washington. On August 28, 1963, 250,000 people traveled to Washington, D.C. They had gathered to show their support for civil rights efforts to end discrimination.

Black and white, they came from the North and the South, the East and the West. They marched through the streets of Washington to the Lincoln Memorial, where civil rights leaders spoke. Dr. Martin Luther King, Jr., one of the speakers, gave his famous "I Have a Dream" speech. In part of that speech, King said: "I have a dream that my four children will one day live in a nation where they will not be judged by the color of their skin, but by the content of their character. . . . I have a dream that one day down in Alabama . . . little black boys and black girls will be able to join hands with little white boys and white girls as brothers and sisters."

The organizers of the march hoped it would convince the United States Congress to pass a new civil rights bill. The new bill would remove discrimination in job opportunities and in public places, such as hotels and restaurants.

Ella Baker did not go to Washington for the march. She knew that it would attract a great deal of attention, and she had never been fond of TV cameras. But there may also have been another reason for her absence. When the march was first planned, no women had been chosen to be a part of the program. Dr. Anna Arnold Hedgeman, the first black woman to be an assistant to a New York City mayor, wrote to A. Philip Randolph, one of the march organizers. In her letter she put pressure on Randolph to include women. Three women who had played a part in the movement were given the opportunity to speak. Since Ella Baker had angered the SCLC when she disagreed with its plan to take over SNCC, it was very unlikely that she would be asked to speak.

"At the March on Washington, she should have been speaking," Bob Moses observed. "She should not have been expected to go there as just another person."

Less than a month later, white hostility to the civil rights movement broke out again. On September 15, a bomb blast

Over 250,000 joined the March on Washington to de-mand civil rights for all.

ripped through a Birmingham church. The bomb killed four young black girls who were attending Bible class. Blacks and whites across the country were once more enraged by an act of southern brutality.

In spite of Bob Moses's experience in McComb, SNCC workers continued to pour into Mississippi. By the end of 1963, they had set up voter-registration offices throughout the state. Now they were ready to move into action for the Freedom Vote campaign.

The Freedom Vote was a mock election that was set up to protest the official elections in which most blacks were not allowed to vote. CORE and SNCC—the two most active groups in COFO—planned the election in order to show that blacks wanted to vote and to give blacks practice in voting. The members of COFO knew that one day blacks would actually vote in real elections and choose real candidates. The Freedom Vote was a step toward that day.

Ella Baker went to Mississippi to help with the project. She spoke at rallies in several Mississippi towns, explaining the purpose of the Freedom Vote and urging blacks to register for it. She had a hand in setting up voting places in black barbershops, beauty parlors, stores, and funeral homes. On voting day, she helped to collect and count the ballots.

Both blacks and whites took part in the Freedom Vote. More than 90,000 cast their ballots. Of that number, more than 80,000 were black. This was four times the number of blacks who were allowed to vote in actual elections.

"What was this doing?" Ella Baker asked. Then she supplied the answer: "This was giving the lie to the old idea that...the reason why Negroes weren't voting was because they weren't interested in voting."

After the Freedom Vote, Ella Baker left Mississippi. But she returned in 1964 to take part in the biggest voter-registration effort of the entire civil rights movement.

TWO MORE SOUTHERN YEARS

" Until the killing of a black mother's son becomes as important as the killing of a white mother's son, we who believe in freedom cannot rest. "

ELLA BAKER

Ella Baker believed that an activist should never relax in the struggle to achieve goals. She encouraged SNCC to push harder in its efforts to register Mississippi blacks to vote. Two major projects in 1964 continued the struggle in Mississippi, and Ella Baker played a key role in one of them. As the first of those projects, COFO planned Freedom Summer. Within COFO, SNCC and CORE members were responsible for carrying out the project. Plans called for Freedom Summer to begin a huge voter-registration drive. It also had another purpose.

For a long time, SNCC workers had complained about not receiving any help from the Federal Bureau of Investigation (FBI) or any other law-enforcement agency. They needed federal protection because they could not count on local police forces. Many southern police officers allowed brutal acts to be committed against SNCC people and sometimes took part in the brutality. SNCC kept a record of how many times civil rights workers in Mississippi had faced life-threatening situations and actual violence. From the end of 1961 to the beginning of 1964, there were 150 such incidents. In most cases, blacks had been the victims of the threats and violence. SNCC felt this was the reason the federal government had made no move to step in, despite many requests to do so.

Some of COFO's leaders believed the government would do something about the violence if the civil rights workers under attack were white. For this reason, they decided to invite white college students from the North to take part in Freedom Summer projects. Whites had worked with SNCC and CORE from the very beginning. But 1964 would be the first time so many were to be involved in an activity that would put them in direct contact with southern whites.

Ella Baker was at the SNCC meeting when this decision was made. She later said: "The Student Nonviolent Coordinating Committee... came to the conclusion that it was a necessary political move to invite white students to participate in the program. They were very aware that when a black person got brutalized for attempting to register to vote, this was nothing new, it had been done before. But when the... daughter and son of people up North... who had some political clout got involved, it was a challenge to the powers that be." Baker did not believe that anyone involved with the decision was inviting white students to join just so they could get beaten and jailed. SNCC looked upon Freedom Summer as a dramatic way of showing the nation that blacks and whites could work together to achieve racial justice. Ella Baker agreed with the decision to include more whites in the movement.

More than 800 white students volunteered for the Freedom Summer project. A special school was set up in Oxford, Ohio, to give them instruction in voter-registration procedures and nonviolent resistance. After a week of training, 300 of the new volunteers left for Mississippi. They arrived on June 20. On June 21, tragedy struck. Three young civil rights workers—James Chaney, Andrew Goodman, and Michael Schwerner—disappeared. Chaney was black; Goodman and Schwerner were white. Andrew Goodman had been among the 300 new volunteers.

This time the federal government took action. Four hundred military men and FBI agents were sent into the South to look for the missing men. On August 4, their bodies were found buried on a farm just outside the town of Philadelphia, Mississippi. They had all been shot to death.

The media gave full coverage to the disappearance of the three young men and the discovery of their bodies. Most Americans were horrified by the stories they read in the papers or saw on their TV screens. A reporter asked Ella Baker to comment on what had happened. She said: "The unfortunate thing is that it took this . . . to make the rest of the country turn its eyes on the fact that there were other [black] bodies lying under the swamps of Mississippi. Until the killing of a black mother's son becomes as important as the killing of a white mother's son, we who believe in freedom cannot rest."

Twenty-one white men, including a county sheriff and a deputy sheriff, were arrested for the murders and brought to trial. The trial took place in a Mississippi courtroom with an all-white jury. After hearing the case, the jury found the men not guilty. All 21 were released. A federal court later tried the case again and sent seven of the men to jail.

Less than a month after Chaney, Goodman, and Schwerner disappeared, the United States Congress and President Lyndon B. Johnson signed the Civil Rights Act of 1964. This bill had

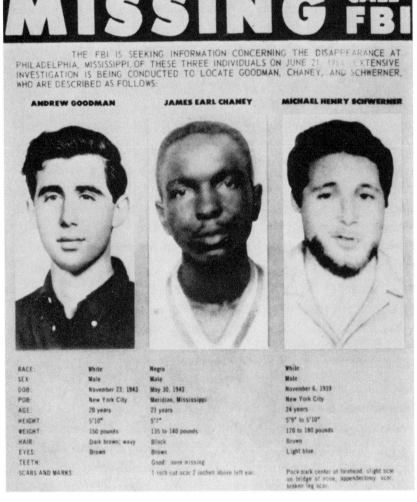

The FBI poster distributed throughout the South during the search for the missing students.

been debated in the House of Representatives and the Senate since the summer of 1963. The main parts of the bill stated that hotels, restaurants, and other public places could not discriminate against blacks. Blacks must have the same opportunities as whites to get jobs, and blacks holding jobs must be given raises and promotions on the same basis that they are given to whites.

And finally, the federal government would help communities to desegregate their schools.

When the 1964 Civil Rights Act became law on July 2, the civil rights movement won a great victory. The law, however, did little for the voting rights of African Americans. That same year, a new amendment to the U.S. Constitution was made. It dealt with voter registration. The 24th Amendment did away with the requirement of having to pay a poll tax in order to vote. But that wasn't enough. There were other obstacles—like literacy tests—that had to be removed before large numbers of blacks could vote. Another law was needed. Until it came along, attempts to register blacks would continue. Some of the white students who had gone to Mississippi for Freedom Summer left the project because of the deaths of their three co-workers. But most of them stayed on. The violence continued, too. Churches were bombed, homes were burned down, and Freedom Summer workers were shot at.

As part of the Freedom Summer project to get the vote for blacks, the Mississippi Freedom Democratic Party (MFDP) was created. For more than 100 years, most white southerners had voted for candidates of the Democratic party. Therefore, the Democratic party was more powerful in the South than the other major party, the Republican party. Like any other political party, the Democratic party decided which candidates it would support and what issues it would take a stand on.

Black Mississippians who were members or supporters of COFO asked the state Democratic party if they could join. The Mississippi Democratic party said no. In response, COFO started a separate political party to represent Mississippi, with membership open to blacks and whites. This was the Mississippi Freedom Democratic Party.

Ella Baker helped to organize the MFDP. It was the third civil rights group that she had had a role in shaping. Soon MFDP offices were established all over Mississippi. Baker was asked to set up and run the MFDP office in Washington, D.C.

In 1964, there would be an election for a new president of the

Ella Baker speaking to delegates of the Mississippi Freedom Democratic Party in Atlantic City.

United States. All the political parties held conventions to choose presidential candidates. Each state sent a delegation of party members to its party's convention, and each delegation took part in selecting the person who would be the party's choice for office.

The Democratic party had its Democratic National Convention in Atlantic City, New Jersey. The regular Mississippi Democratic delegation that went to the convention was all-white. The MFDP was there, too, and its members challenged the all-white delegation. In its challenge, the MFDP argued that the Mississippi delegation didn't represent all the people of the state. There were no blacks in the Mississippi Democratic party and no blacks in the delegation. The MFDP was interracial, and could speak for black as well as white Mississippians. The MFDP therefore asked the convention to allow its members to be Mississippi's official delegation.

Ella Baker and other members of the MFDP knew that the

Fannie Lou Hamer spoke out for civil rights at the Democratic National Convention in 1964.

new party wouldn't be able to fight the battle alone. It needed the help of people who could influence convention officials. Baker knew members of Congress from Michigan, New York, California, Pennsylvania, and several other states. She spoke with them, and they agreed to support the MFDP's attempt to replace Mississippi's all-white delegation.

One of the most moving moments at the convention took place when the vice chairperson of the MFDP, Fannie Lou Hamer, spoke to the delegates. Mrs. Hamer had been involved in voter-registration activities since 1962, when she went to a SNCC meeting in her hometown of Ruleville, Mississippi. When she tried to register, Hamer was fired from her job as a timekeeper on a large plantation where the land was farmed by sharecroppers. Later, in another attempt to register, Hamer was arrested by Mississippi police and brutally beaten.

Hamer's speech to the convention was carried to the entire nation by TV. As she was telling the delegates about being beaten, Hamer suddenly disappeared from the screen and President Lyndon Johnson appeared. President Johnson, a Democrat, expected to be nominated for president again by his party. He thought that Hamer's statements would cause him to lose votes in the South, so he ordered that she be cut off. (As president of the United States, Johnson had the power to interrupt any TV program if he had an official announcement to make.)

President Johnson tried to assure the nation that the convention would be peaceful, but he did not succeed in preventing millions of people from finding out about Fannie Lou Hamer's beating. While he was on TV, cameras at the convention continued to record what Hamer had to say. Later that evening, her statement was broadcast on news programs nationwide. Thousands of people called the convention to express their anger over Hamer's terrible beating and the president's attempt to keep the

Fannie Lou Hamer (center), Ella Baker (right), and others sing a freedom song outside the Convention.

people of the United States from finding out about it.

The question of whether the MFDP would represent Mississippi was handled by two leaders of the Democratic party— Hubert Humphrey, vice president of the United States, and Walter Mondale, who was then attorney general of the state of Minnesota. They suggested that two MFDP members be named as delegates to the convention. These two would not be part of Mississippi's delegation, but they could participate in convention activities. The MFDP turned down their offer.

In a way, the MFDP lost the fight against the state party at the convention that year. In the long run, however, the MFDP won. The national Democratic party established a new requirement for future conventions: All state delegations would have to be racially mixed. All the same, MFDP members weren't happy about the way they had been treated at the convention. They left Atlantic City feeling that democracy hadn't worked for them.

After spending a couple of weeks at the MFDP office in Washington, D.C., Ella Baker returned to Atlanta to work with SNCC and SCEF. MFDP members, along with Freedom Summer volunteers, continued their voter-registration work in Mississippi throughout 1964 and into the following year. But in 1965, the fight for the right to vote received the most attention in Alabama.

SNCC had begun a voter-registration program in Selma, Alabama, in 1963. Like SNCC workers elsewhere in the South, those in Selma were beaten and jailed. The situation took an even more violent turn in 1965, when Dr. King and the SCLC joined forces with SNCC. Hundreds of blacks, including King, were arrested and sent to prison. Just as in Birmingham two years earlier, teenagers and children marched in the demonstrations. The Selma police, like those in Birmingham, arrested the children, along with the adults.

To dramatize the need for voting rights for African Americans and to pressure Congress into passing a voting-rights bill, the SCLC planned a march from Selma to Alabama's capital at Montgomery. It is a distance of slightly more than 50 miles and would take at least five days to complete on foot.

On Sunday, March 7, 1965, Hosea Williams of the SCLC and John Lewis of SNCC led 600 people out of Selma and headed toward Montgomery. The march was stopped by an Alabama state trooper at the Edmund Pettus Bridge. Behind him stood a column of fellow troopers equipped with gas masks and billy clubs. There were others on horseback.

When Lewis and Williams asked to speak with him, the trooper ordered his men to attack. They moved in, knocking marchers to the ground. Some threw cans that filled the air with thick clouds of tear gas. Troopers on horses rushed in and struck with their clubs, chasing the blacks away from the bridge.

Eight-year-old Sheyann Webb was one of the children in the march. "All I could see was the outburst of tear gas," she later recalled. "I saw people being beaten and I tried to run home as fast as I could. And as I began to run home, I saw horses behind me.... Hosea Williams picked me up and I told him to put me down, he wasn't running fast enough."

That day became known as Bloody Sunday. Scenes of Bloody Sunday appeared nationwide in the media. Hundreds of people—both blacks and whites—began to pour into Selma to take part in the next march. The SCLC went to the federal court to get the right to march to Montgomery. Even though the court had not yet decided on the SCLC's right to march, King decided to march anyway. He didn't want to lose the hundreds of people who had come to walk with him to Montgomery.

On Tuesday, March 9, about 1,500 marchers set out. This time King took the lead. The walk to Montgomery was again halted by Alabama state troopers at the bridge. Because he wanted no violence, King turned the demonstrators around and led them back into Selma.

The Selma-Montgomery March

In February, 1965, 26-year-old Jimmy Lee Jackson was killed by Alabama state police. Jackson had been trying to protect his mother and his 82-year-old grandfather from being beaten during a demonstration for voting rights. Albert Turner, a local civil rights leader, said that African Americans were so angry that "we wanted to carry Jimmy's body to [Governor] George Wallace." Instead, they decided to march from Selma to Montgomery, the state capital. The first attempt was brutally stopped. State troopers on horses threw tear gas at protesters, knocked them down, and beat them. On the third try, 4,000 people of all races and religions and all walks of life set out. Five days and 54 miles later, 25,000 marchers reached Montgomery. A few days after this, President Johnson announced that he was sending a voting rights bill to Congress. The bill would "strike down all restrictions used to deny to people the right to vote."

Martin Luther King, Jr., leads the historic march.

Montgomery police at the state capitol building, ready to confront the marchers from Selma.

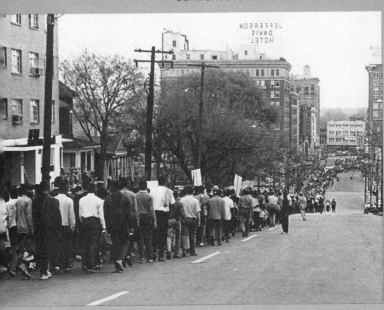

Marchers from Selma pass through Montgomery on their way to confront Governor George Wallace.

On March 16, the SCLC received good news from the federal court. The court ruled that a march from Selma to Montgomery would be legal. Four thousand people gathered in Selma to march on Sunday, March 21. President Johnson put the Alabama National Guard under his authority and ordered them to protect the marchers. He also sent in 2,000 army troops and 200 FBI agents and federal marshals.

Again, Dr. King led the march. Along the way, others fell in with those who had started out. By the time they reached the outskirts of Montgomery, the number of marchers had swelled to 25,000. They marched through the streets of Montgomery on Thursday, March 25.

Although John Lewis had been a leader in the first attempt to walk to Montgomery, many SNCC members weren't in favor of the march. They thought it was too dangerous. On the open road to Montgomery, the marchers would be easy targets for white violence. SNCC workers were willing to risk their own lives, but not the lives of the hundreds of people who would take part in the march. The march caused so much disagreement among SNCC members that this might explain why Ella Baker wasn't there.

The Selma march and all the other efforts to get the vote for southern blacks finally paid off. On August 6, 1965, the Voting Rights Act became law. The act dealt with literacy tests as part of voter registration. It didn't eliminate them completely, but it did limit where they could be used. The tests could not be given in states where less than 50 percent of those eligible to vote had been registered. This was true of six southern states—Alabama, Georgia, Louisiana, Mississippi, South Carolina, and Virginia. Parts of North Carolina also had to put an end to literacy tests.

The civil rights movement achieved major goals with the Civil Rights Act of 1964 and the Voting Rights Act of 1965. Unfortunately, these two laws did not end discrimination against blacks. However, most discrimination was no longer legal, as it had been under Jim Crow laws. Even today, African Americans continue to fight for equal rights.

Shortly after the Voting Rights Act was passed, Ella Baker left Atlanta and returned to her home in Harlem. She had generously contributed her skills and knowledge to the movement, and had seen it achieve success. The lives of blacks as well as whites were changed for the better. The United States moved closer to keeping its promise of justice and democracy for all.

EPILOGUE

❝ People have to be made to understand that they cannot look for salvation anywhere but to themselves....Every time I see a young person who... identifies...with the struggle of black people...I take new hope. I feel a new life as a result of it. ❞

ELLA BAKER

Back in New York City, Ella Baker continued her activities in SNCC, the MFDP, and SCEF. For several years, she traveled to the South for meetings with the MFDP and SCEF, and to Illinois, where SNCC had set up a new office.

Although the MFDP had failed to replace the all-white Mississippi delegation at the Democratic National Convention in 1964, it remained active in Mississippi politics. In 1967, MFDP candidates won elections for sheriff, school-board members, and other public offices in a number of Mississippi towns. Today blacks are able to join the state's regular Democratic party, so the MFDP no longer exists. SCEF had worked hard to improve relations between southern blacks and whites. By the end of the 1960s, many of SCEF's goals had been reached. In the 1970s, it also went out of existence.

In 1966, Stokely Carmichael became SNCC's chairman. He had been with SNCC for five years, mainly working with voter registration in Mississippi. As chairman, Carmichael made many changes in SNCC. The group gave up its goal of racial integration and instead pushed for black power. "Black power" was a slogan used by many African Americans who felt that blacks should be independent of whites in the United States. Black power meant that blacks should take pride in their culture and their identity. They should develop and rely on their own businesses and schools, and establish their own political parties. In the book *Black Power*, which Stokely Carmichael wrote with Charles Hamilton, there is this statement: "Black Power...is a call for black people in this country to unite, to recognize their [African] heritage, to build a sense of community. It is a call for black people...to define their own goals, to lead their own organizations. It is a call to reject the racist institutions and values of this society."

Ella Baker believed that members of SNCC turned to black power because they were disappointed by an American democracy that didn't work for blacks. SNCC volunteers had risked their lives in Mississippi. They felt betrayed when the Democratic convention refused to allow the MFDP to represent Mississippi. Many SNCC staff workers and volunteers had left college to devote themselves completely to the movement. In spite of the civil rights laws of 1964 and 1965, they felt that more needed to be done. But white America didn't seem willing to do any more.

In a 1968 interview, Ella Baker made these observations: "Part of it [black power] sprang from the frustrations of having given so much and...having had faith that the democratic process would provide certain types of things and it didn't....[SNCC developed the] belief that the only answer is a more revolution-ary approach. . . . This is what people have been driven to, even an older person like me who has been around all these years."

SNCC's demand for black power was one of the main reasons the unity of the movement began to break down. Although CORE joined SNCC in calling for black independence, the NAACP and the SCLC did not. After 1965, these four leading civil rights organizations never again worked together in a major civil rights effort. By 1990, there was only a weak version of CORE, and SNCC no longer existed. Only the NAACP and the SCLC remained active.

From the Montgomery bus boycott of 1955 to the Voting Rights Act of 1965, the civil rights movement was significant for African Americans, particularly those in the South. There, millions of African Americans were able to register and vote for the first time. They became actively involved in the politics of the South and the nation. Jobs that were once closed to them opened up. Stores, parks, libraries, and other public facilities were no longer segregated. And perhaps most important of all, the civil rights movement gave all African Americans a sense of pride in being black.

When Ella Baker was asked about the effect of the movement on blacks, she responded: "People are more easily alerted to whether they are getting oppression [unfair treatment because of race], and they'll do something. They're quicker to respond now. They would be much less willing to settle for what they had endured before."

In New York, Ella Baker again took up her work with com-munity groups that were seeking better housing and job oppor-tunites for Harlem's blacks. During the early 1970s, Baker's desire to help people in their fight for freedom stretched to a new continent. She became involved in the struggle of black Africans against white rule in Rhodesia. Although blacks there made up most of the population, they could not vote in their country's elections. They were discriminated against in educa-

African Americans in Selma, Alabama, line up for voter registration numbers.

tion, housing, and jobs. To raise money for the freedom fighters in Rhodesia, Ella Baker helped to organize rallies and even held events in her Harlem home. The blacks in Rhodesia eventually succeeded in removing whites from power. In 1980, Rhodesia became Zimbabwe, with a government that was now run by blacks.

Ella Baker also worked for the freedom struggle in South Africa. There blacks are forced to live under a system of extreme racial segregation known as apartheid. The country is mostly black, but under white rule, blacks have no say in the government. Their opportunities for decent jobs and good education are limited. They can live only in certain areas. The situation for blacks in South Africa is much the same as it was for blacks in Rhodesia.

South Africa is a larger and more powerful country than Rhodesia was. This could be the reason why the black struggle there has gone on so long. The leading black South African freedom organization is the African National Congress (ANC), which was formed in 1912. Through peaceful means, such as negotiations with the government and strikes by workers, the ANC hoped to have apartheid removed. When these efforts did not succeed, the ANC turned to violence during the early 1960s. It cut telephone lines and blew up railroad tracks and empty government buildings. The ANC's leader, Nelson Mandela, was held responsible for these acts of violence. He was arrested, and in 1963 Mandela was sent to prison for life. Also, the government prevented the ANC from operating in South Africa. Although the ANC now had its headquarters outside of South Africa, it continued to be a major influence on the efforts of South African blacks to gain their freedom. In 1990, Nelson Mandela was released from jail, and the ANC was allowed to return to South Africa. The struggle for freedom went on.

As she had done for the blacks of Zimbabwe, Ella Baker raised money to continue the fight for racial equality in South Africa. Members of the ANC often visited New York. Baker met with them and introduced them to other blacks and whites who might be able to help the ANC's cause.

Closer to home, Ella Baker served on the board of directors of the Puerto Rican Solidarity Committee. Most of the men and women of the committee were not Puerto Ricans. They were Americans who supported Puerto Rico's independence from the United States. Spain had at one time governed Puerto Rico. But after the Spanish-American War, Puerto Rico became a U.S. possession. Since 1900, Puerto Rico has developed its own government, elected by its own people, and today the island is called an associated state. It is officially called a commonwealth. Its people are citizens of the United States, and it has a representative in the United States Congress. That representative speaks for Puerto Rico but cannot vote on issues that come up in Congress. Puerto Rico is, therefore, somewhat independent from the United States. However, there are Puerto Ricans, such

Ella Baker was a great behind-the-scenes leader in the civil rights movement.

as those supported by the Puerto Rican Solidarity Committee, who want complete independence.

During her later years, Ella Baker began to receive the kind of attention she had always tried to avoid. To celebrate her 75th birthday in 1978, the city of New York had a party in her honor. In 1984, she was presented with a Candace Award for outstanding achievement by the Coalition of 100 Black Women. Her old friends Rosa Parks from Montgomery and Daisy Bates from Little Rock were also awarded Candaces.

When Ella Baker died in New York City on December 13, 1986, her importance to the civil rights movement was recognized nationally. Through her, thousands of black southerners had found the courage to join the NAACP and to make contribution to the struggle of African Americans for freedom. The SCLC was shaped by her ability to organize. Under her gentle guidance, SNCC developed into one of the strongest forces in the civil rights movement. With her help, the MFDP became a voice that spoke for the blacks of Mississippi. Baker was like needle and thread, sewing together the different parts of the movement.

Ella Baker has been an inspiration to many who have dedicated themselves to serving the needs of others. Today she is a role model for both white and black women. Her life has shown that women have the power and the intelligence to make significant changes in the way large numbers of people live and think.

The names of Ella Baker and Nelson Mandela have been joined to form the title of a student movement against racism: the Baker/Mandela Institute. Established at the University of Michigan, the institute will give young people a chance to study racial prejudice and explore ways of putting an end to it.

"I believe that the struggle is eternal," Ella Baker said. "Somebody else carries on." With her own life, and through the efforts and achievements of the many people whom she has inspired, the example of Ella Baker does carry on—to make the world a better place for all of us.

Timetable of Events
in the Life of
Ella Baker

Dec. 13, 1903	Born in Norfolk, Virginia
1911	Moves to North Carolina
1918	Enters Shaw University in Raleigh, North Carolina
1927	Graduates from Shaw University Moves to Harlem in New York City
1936	Accepts a position with Works Progress Administration (WPA)
1938	Begins working with National Association for the Advancement of Colored People (NAACP)
1942	Named director of NAACP's offices (branches) nationwide
1954	Becomes president of New York City branch of NAACP
1958	Helps organize Southern Christian Leadership Conference (SCLC)
1960	Paves the way for creation of Student Nonviolent Coordinating Committee (SNCC) and becomes its advisor
1964	Helps organize Mississippi Freedom Democratic Party (MFDP)
Dec. 13, 1986	Dies in New York City

SUGGESTED READING

Branch, Taylor. *Parting the Waters: America in the King Years, 1954–63*. New York: Simon and Schuster, 1988.

Brown, Cynthia, and Septima Clarke. *Ready from Within*. Navarro: Wild Trees Press, 1986.

*Davidson, Margaret. *I Have a Dream: The Story of Martin Luther King, Jr.* New York, Scholastic, 1986.

*Du Bois, W.E.B. *The Souls of Black Folk*. New York: Dodd Mead, 1979.

Garrow, David. *Bearing the Cross: Martin Luther King Jr., and the Southern Christian Leadership Conference*. New York: William Morrow, 1986.

*McKissack, Patricia, and Frederick McKissack. *The Civil Rights Movement in America from 1865 to the Present*. Chicago: Childrens Press, 1987.

Morris, Aldon. *Origins of the Civil Rights Movement*. New York: The Free Press, 1984.

Raines, Howell. *My Soul Is Rested: The Story of the Civil Rights Movement in the Deep South*. New York: Penguin, 1983.

*Rollins, Charlemae H. *They Showed the Way: Forty American Negro Leaders*. New York: Crowell, 1964.

*Ross, H. K. *Black American Women, No. 3*. Scarsdale, N.Y.: Lion Books, 1988.

Williams, Juan. *Eyes on the Prize*. New York: Viking, 1987.

---

*Readers of *Ella Baker: A Leader Behind the Scenes* will find these books particularly readable.

SOURCES

BOOKS

Blumberg, Rhoda Goldstein. *Civil Rights: The 1960s Freedom Struggle*. Boston: Twayne Publishers, 1984.

Brooks, Thomas R. *Walls Come Tumbling Down*. Englewood Cliffs, N.J.: Prentice-Hall, 1974.

Cantarow, Ellen, and Susan Gushee O'Malley. *Moving the Mountain*. Old Westbury, N.Y.: The Feminist Press, 1980.

Carson, Clayborne. *In Struggle: SNCC and the Black Awakening of the 1960s*. Cambridge, Mass.: Harvard University Press, 1981.

Carter, Wilmoth A. *Shaw's Universe: A Monument to Educational Innovation*. Rockville, Md.: D.C. National Publishing, 1973.

Davidson, Margaret. *I Have a Dream: The Story of Martin Luther King*. New York: Scholastic, 1986.

Forman, James. *The Making of Black Revolutionaries*. New York: Macmillan, 1972.

Garrow, David. *Bearing the Cross: Martin Luther King Jr., and the Southern Christian Leadership Conference*. New York: William Morrow, 1986.

Giddings, Paula. *When and Where I Enter: The Impact of Black Women on Race and Sex in America*. New York: William Morrow, 1984.

Lerner, Gerda, ed. *Black Women in White America*. New York: Pantheon, 1972.

Lincoln, C. Eric, ed. *Martin Luther King, Jr.* New York: Hill and Wang, 1984.

Morris, Aldon. *The Origins of the Civil Rights Movement*. New York: The Free Press, 1984.

Myrdal, Gunnar, *An American Dilemma*. New York: Harper and Row, 1962.

Raines, Howell. *My Soul Is Rested: Movement Days in the Deep South*. New York: Penguin, 1983.

Watters, Pat, and Reese Claghorn. *Climbing Jacob's Ladder: The Arrival of Negroes in Southern Politics*. New York: Harcourt, Brace and World, 1967.

Williams, Juan. *Eyes on the Prize*. New York: Viking, 1987.

Woodward, C. Vann. *The Strange Career of Jim Crow:* New York: Oxford University Press, 1974.

NEWSPAPER ARTICLES

The New York Times. 8/7/64, 11/8/84, 12/17/86.

MAGAZINE ARTICLES

American Visions (Obituary), February 1987.

Baker, Ella. "Bigger Than a Hamburger." *Southern Patriot*, June 1960.

Christian Century (Obituary), January 1987.

Fuller, Helen. "Southern Students Take Over." *The New Republic*, May 2, 1960.

Fuller, Helen. "We Are All So Very Happy." *The New Republic*, April 25, 1960.

Jet (Obituary), January 19, 1987.

"NAACP, SCLC, SNCC: Ella Baker Got Them Moving." *Ms.*, June 1980.

INTERVIEWS

Baker, Ella. Interview by John Britton, 1968. The Civil Rights Documentation Project of the Moorland-Spingarn Collection, Howard University.

Brockington, Jacqueline Baker. Interview with author, June 29, 1989.

Guyot, Lawrence. Interview with author, September 14, 1989.

Moses, Robert. Interview with author, July 25, 1989.

Shuttlesworth, Rev. Fred. Interview with author, October 8, 1989.

OTHER

Grant, Joanne. *Fundi: The Story of Ella Baker.* Franklin Lakes, N.J.: New Day Films, 1981. Film.

The Schomburg Center for Research in Black Culture, Symposium on the Mississippi Summer Project, June 29, 1989.

INDEX

About the Author

Shyrlee Dallard began her 12-year career as a television producer-writer in Philadelphia. Six of those years were spent at the Children's Television Workshop, where she was a live-action film producer for *Sesame Street*. A graduate of Smith College, Ms. Dallard is now a full-time free-lance writer.

Text Permissions:

Poem on page 26 copyright 1926 by Alfred A. Knopf Inc. and renewed 1954 by Langston Hughes. Reprinted from *Selected Poems of Langston Hughes*, by permission of Alfred A. Knopf Inc.

Excerpts from *Moving the Mountain: Women for Social Change* by Ellen Cantarow with Susan Gushee O'Malley and Sharon Hartman Strom. Copyright © 1980 by The Feminist Press at The City University of New York. Reprinted by permission. All rights reserved.

From *The Making of Black Revolutionaries* by James Forman. Reprinted by permission of Open Hand Publishing, Inc.

From *The Wretched of the Earth* by Frantz Fanon. Copyright © 1963 by Présence Africaine. Used by permission of Grove Weidenfeld.

From the film series *Eyes on the Prize: America's Civil Rights Years, 1954-1965*. Copyright © 1987 by Blackside, Inc. All Rights Reserved. Reprinted by Permission.

From *Eyes on the Prize: America's Civil Rights Years, 1954-1965* by Juan Williams and the Eyes On The Prize production team. Published by Viking-Penguin. Copyright © 1987 by Blackside, Inc. Reprinted with permission of Blackside, Inc.

From *Black Women in White America* by Gerda Lerner. Copyright © 1972 by Gerda Lerner. Reprinted by permission of Random House, Inc.

Picture Credits: AP/Wide World Photos: 34, 44, 51, 60, 67, 73, 85, 95, 108, 113; George Ballis: 107, 109; Magnum/Eliott Erwitt: 10; Magnum/Danny Lyon: cover portrait, 121; Bert Miles: 100; Moorland-Spingarn Research Center: 7; Robert Sengstacke: 113; Schomburg Center for Research in Black Culture, N.Y. Public Library, Astor, Lenox and Tilden Foundations: cover background, 28, 29, 105; UPI/Bettmann: 87, 112.

4/92

03 ADAMS PARK

J B BAKER   APB
Dallard, Shyrlee
Ella Baker

Atlanta-Fulton Public Library